Achieving Fair Value

How Companies Can Better Manage Their
Relationships with Investors

Mark C. Scott

John Wiley & Sons, Ltd

Other Wiley Editorial Offices

John Wiley & Sons Inc., 111 River Street, Hoboken, NJ 07030, USA

Jossey-Bass, 989 Market Street, San Francisco, CA 94103-1741, USA

Wiley-VCH Verlag GmbH, Boschstr. 12, D-69469 Weinheim, Germany

John Wiley & Sons Australia Ltd, 33 Park Road, Milton, Queensland 4064, Australia

John Wiley & Sons (Asia) Pte Ltd, 2 Clementi Loop #02-01, Jin Xing Distripark, Singapore 129809

John Wiley & Sons Canada Ltd, 22 Worcester Road, Etobicoke, Ontario, Canada M9W 1L1

Wiley also publishes its books in a variety of electronic formats. Some content that appears
in print may not be available in electronic books.

British Library Cataloguing in Publication Data

A catalogue record for this book is available from the British Library

ISBN 0-470-02390-2

Project management by Originator, Gt Yarmouth, Norfolk (typeset in 11/16pt Trump Medieval)
Printed and bound in Great Britain by Antony Rowe Ltd, Chippenham, Wiltshire
This book is printed on acid-free paper responsibly manufactured from sustainable forestry
in which at least two trees are planted for each one used for paper production.

Contents

Acknowledgements   v

The fair value process   vi

Introduction: What is "fair value" and why does it
    matter?   1

Part One: The Imperative for a Fair Value Strategy   7

1   Getting the goals right   9
    What should management be trying to achieve
    on behalf of shareholders?

2   Why do the markets get it wrong?   21
    Why do markets fail to identify fair value?

3   Understanding the institutional fund manager   47
    Why do fund managers behave as they do and
    what can management do about it?

Part Two: The Building Blocks of Fair Value   69

4   Towards a fair value strategy   71
    Understanding the fair value process

5   Determining fair value   81
    How do you know when your company is
    fairly valued?

6   Targeting value-determining investors   119
    Identifying the shareholders that matter

7   Profiling value-determining investors   135
    Getting to know the culprits

Part Three: Delivering a Fair Value Strategy   147

8   Towards fair value levers   149
    Knowing a good lever from a bad lever

9   Deciding how much to tell investors   163
    When ignorance is not bliss

10 Deciding how to tell investors   187
    The art of managing communications channels

11 The role of management quality   201
    Setting the fair value context

Part Four: The Challenge of Managing for Fair Value 221

12 Managing a fair value strategy   223
    The challenge of coordination

13 What to expect from the next decade   231

Bibliography   238

Index   242

Acknowledgements

THIS BOOK WOULD NOT HAVE BEEN POSSIBLE WITHOUT the support of the Ashridge Strategic Management Centre and the input of its directors and associates. Thanks are due in particular to Andrew Campbell and Michael Goold who have patiently helped guide the thinking behind the concept of fair value from its beginnings, through a lengthy research programme, to the final concept. The observations and insights detailed in this book have been gleaned through the input of a wide number of professionals involved in the investor relations (IR) process and also from the fund management and investment banking industry. Detailed interviews and analysis have been conducted with a large group of public companies and, in respect of the price-sensitive nature of many of their contributions, their names have been omitted from the text. Finally, I also owe a debt of thanks to Angela Munro, without whom I would have driven the production department of John Wiley & Sons to the brink of despair.

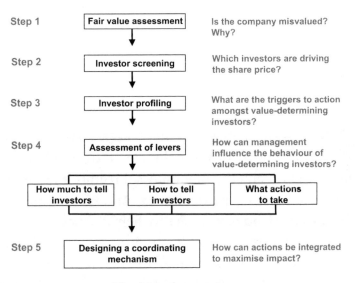

The fair value process.

Introduction: What is "fair value" and why does it matter?

I F YOU ASK CEOS OF LARGE PUBLIC COMPANIES WHAT IS THE most demanding aspect of their job, you are likely to get one answer – managing the relationship with the financial markets and investors. It is an extraordinary answer if you think about it. You might expect the demanding thing to be managing the business itself – dealing with tough customers, with demanding employees, with capital allocation issues, with cashflow. But dealing with the financial markets absorbs on average 25% of the time of the CEO and up to 35% of the attention of the CFO. That is the single largest drain on the most valuable resource the company possesses.

This in itself should sound a few alarm bells. Is attention being focused where it should be? What about corporate strategy, what about operations, what about marketing and HR – all those areas that management literature tells us are the business essentials? Is there something innately inefficient about the way large companies handle their relationship with investors and with the capital markets? A few influential titans, such as Intel, Coke and HP, have, in public at least, declared this is not where valuable time should be spent. But, for the vast majority of large quoted companies, it remains the single biggest drain on senior time.

To help them in the battle for fund manager support, most corporates have built up an investor relations function. This is typically comprised of an Investor Relations (IR) director plus a couple of analysts, whose primary role is to manage the large logistics exercise of interacting with institutional fund managers. They also retain a house broker, supported by the lead analyst, to help market the shares to existing and prospective investors. This is often supplemented by external IR advisors, PR strategists and a range of additional eyes and ears on the institutional marketplace. The average direct time and fee cost for a FTSE 250 company is probably in excess of £2m and a multiple of this if the indirect time costs of top management are accounted for.

The primary reason management are prepared to invest so much time managing the relationship with the financial markets is because it is the movement of the shareprice that determines whether they are seen to be winning or failing. The primary modern measure of successful management is the ability to maximise shareprice. The manager who succeeds, for a sustained period of time, to maximise shareprice receives universal accolades. They are the darlings of the City and Wall Street and they are rewarded accordingly. It is no longer sufficient to focus internally on long-term strategies to deliver earnings and revenue growth. Managers are required and incentivised to maximise the value attached to their efforts by the financial markets.

Yet, despite the resources committed to it, the battle to maximise shareprice is one that so few companies appear able to win at for long. The typical pattern of larger groups is shareprice boom and bust – historically over a 7-year cycle. Over the past decade the FTSE 100 and Dow Jones Industrial Average have on average suffered an annual 20% volatility – the average difference between their highs and lows on a moving 12-month basis. This is immensely disruptive to the businesses concerned, driving endless shifts in strategy and management. The average CEO's tenure is now down to 3 years, shorter than the classic strategy cycle of 5 years. As a result, both the strategy process and management are highly geared to managing and meeting market perceptions. This can and often does lead to distortions of behaviour, or what is labelled "short-termism".

The blame for this short-termism is usually put on the shoulders of "the market" and is in particular credited to the short time horizon of institutional fund managers. This suspicion has been so strong in the UK, for example, that the government has actually launched an enquiry to look into the sources of institutional short-termism.As this book will explore, the markets and institutional fund managers may be far from perfect. But much of the challenge lies with the way businesses manage their relationships with financial markets and investors. This book contests that it is ultimately within the power of executive teams to better manage their relationships with fund managers, with more effective use of their most valuable resource, by applying new approaches to the IR function. This book proposes a constructive way to reduce shareprice volatility and investor churn.

The concept of "fair value" is a simple one – that an appropriate strategy for management is to ensure that their business is fairly valued. In other words, to ensure that its market value accurately reflects the business's fundamental, sustainable worth. In some cases this may imply that management need to actively manage down situations of overvaluation. But, more generally, fair value means that the primary focus of management should be on fundamental, operational value creation and ensuring that this is as accurately valued by investors as possible. The idea of fair value often requires a major change of mindset on the part of management for whom share value maximisation is deeply ingrained. It also requires a change in the relationship the company maintains with its brokers, the analysts that follow the company and other advisors.

Pursuing a fair value strategy demands the development of a set of analytical tools and management processes which are typically underdeveloped in most companies. Most IR functions are not ideally equipped to undertake fundamental analysis of the share register, to identify active fund managers that might be setting the shareprice and to predict investor behaviour. Nor are they usually well equipped to provide detailed guidance on valuation. The fair value approach also requires the development of a set of skills and coordination ability at the corporate parent level which are often not present. Investor relations cannot operate as a stand-alone activity reporting to the CFO. It has to be a coordination function between corporate strategy, finance and the executive, focused on long-term valuation, analysis of the share register, and proactive management of investor perceptions. In this coordinating role it is one of the most important parenting functions at the corporate centre.

In the process of researching this book, I have been surprised how little strategic insight has been developed in the area of managing relationships with investors. The investor relations function itself has only been in existence for around 15 years, and hence is a relatively new discipline. It is typically not integrated with the strategy function which has an older heritage. Unlike strategy, there is virtually no academic or consulting wisdom on the subject. There are no robust strategic frameworks to guide management action. It has evolved through expediency and without design. The role of the IR director is not a board role, nor does it usually represent a genuine career avenue in its own right. Instead, this critical area of expertise remains largely outsourced to the broker community. It is now time that it was brought squarely in-house as a core competence.

This book is intended to provide a practical introduction to each of the core elements of fair value strategy and improve the ability of the company to manage its institutional investors. It is equally relevant for the IR director seeking to refine their approach to managing investors, or for a management team that senses they can improve their effectiveness or who believe they are currently being misvalued. It is the ability of corporate executives to manage their institutional investors that will determine whether they are perceived to have succeeded or failed.

Part One

The Imperative for a Fair Value Strategy

1

Getting the goals right

What should management be trying to achieve on behalf of shareholders?

IF YOU ASK ANY OWNER-MANAGER OF A PRIVATE COMPANY what is their ultimate mission, the answer will be simple – to maximise the wealth created for them by the business. What do they mean by this? On the whole they will not have thought through the concept of "wealth" with much precision. But what they usually mean is managing the business in a way that maximises profitability and cashflow and therefore return on the equity they have invested in it. In other words, their root concern will be fundamental performance.

If you ask the same question of corporate-level managers of large quoted businesses you may get a subtly different answer. They will talk of maximising shareholder value – another term for shareholder wealth. But what they will mean is maximising shareprice, not necessarily fundamental performance. There is an important distinction between the two – one relates to how the markets perceive future performance potential, and hence stimulate demand for the shares, and the other relates to actual performance that has been and can continue to be achieved. The two notions continually diverge, often for long periods of time, and for a wide array of potential reasons.

Almost every corporate-level manager of a public company is uniquely focused on maximising shareprice. This is how performance is measured. It is also how performance is rewarded. The pursuit of maximum shareprice is deeply rooted in the management psyche and for good reason – that is how investors categorise stocks. Quoted stocks are implicitly ranked by market capitalisation. On the basis of their "market cap" they are grouped into indices, whether the FTSE 100, the Dow Jones Industrial Average or the S&P 500. Around 50% of large-cap institutional fund managers rely explicitly on index-based investment strategies of one sort or another to drive the "weighting" of their portfolios. Within these indices large stocks will typically be highly dominant. Whether a firm is in an index or not has a critical influence on the valuation attached to it and hence there is an immense incentive to get into and remain in an index. Movement in or out of an index can make or break a management team.[1]

In a sense, this is nothing new. Managers have always had a keen eye on shareprice. But the intensity of the focus on maximising shareprice appears to have sharpened. In the

---

[1] An exit from a major index is typically met with an immediate 3% fall in shareprice on the day of announcement. But a much larger fall has typically been built into the shareprice for some time in expectation that the company will exit the index.

wake of the development of increasingly deep, deregulated and accessible markets over the last 20 years, the shareprice objective has received a shot in the arm. The number of eager market participants has exploded, both through direct dealing as well as through institutionally managed funds. The rise of indexation amongst institutional fund managers has also crystallised attention on market cap and short-term shareprice. Expectations of investor returns have grown.

The sources of this mounting pressure to maximise share values are subtle and we will examine them in detail. Part of it comes from the changing nature of the institutional investor base, part of it from the incentives and influence of market intermediaries, principally the brokerage arms of investment banks. Part of it stems from the motivations of management themselves. Even academia has been in on the act. Techniques such as Value Based Management have explicitly linked the management process to the maximisation of share value, something about which I will have much to say presently. The unstated but ubiquitous clamour to inflate the market cap of any large quoted company has been universal.

Is setting a goal of shareprice maximisation a sure route to maximising total shareholder returns or "TSR"?[2] Our research would suggest not. The problem with shareprice is that it can become de-coupled from fundamental performance. This can happen for a large number of reasons. A sector can suddenly become "hot", a company can attract

---

[2] TSR is the sum of capital appreciation per share, plus dividends paid per share.

disproportionate attention in the belief it will transform itself, particular fund managers may perceive an arbitrage opportunity in a sector, or an entire market may enter a period of acceleration. In these situations, the company may begin to attract a premium to its underlying fundamental value. Often such a premium is hard to pin down and management may strenuously deny to themselves and everyone else that there is a premium at all. Even the most objective value investor may find it hard to recognise whether a valuation is inappropriate or not. Besides, isn't the pursuit of a premium what it is all about anyway?

Enter the misvaluation trap

The premium cycle typically works like this: the company succeeds in capturing the attention of the capital markets, perhaps by virtue of a change of management or a takeover or some other significant event. Its advisors will have a large incentive to see the company's stock come to life. Brokers will begin to sense there may be momentum in the stock from which they can glean attractive commissions. Suddenly the company will begin getting increased coverage by the sell-side analysts they employ. Perhaps the company is in a position to become a sector consolidator, perhaps there is the chance for a further major acquisition. Soon the company is being visited by teams of investment bankers who can sense potential deal flow. In order to finance this new burst of activity the company has to issue new stock either through a "rights issue" or a general capital-raising process, all creating commissions for the brokers and corporate financiers. Prompted by the "house broker",[3] new institutional fund managers start increasing their weightings, quickly followed by more passive institutional fund managers. Suddenly the company has the rated stock to execute grander plans.

As this activity cycle deepens, all attention shifts to capitalising on the shareprice. The HR consultants descend with exotic senior management incentive schemes. Large option grants are made to enable management to "align" their interests with those of investors. Debt levels are raised to fund deals which increase earnings per share through the effects of leverage, even if the deals themselves are struck at high multiples of earnings. The CEO and CFO suddenly find themselves spending 50% of their time interacting with the financial community in one shape or another. The financial PR consultants work overtime to maximise the column inches attributed to the company in the press, and in the process the CEO and CFO are given large amounts of personal coverage. They are elevated to the dais of corporate players. The net effect is that perceptions are created that high, almost certainly double-digit growth rates can be delivered indefinitely, even if the company is very large indeed.

In this premium-building process, an extraordinary thing has happened. The company has begun to have a life on the capital markets that is effectively divorced from its real life, from its underlying performance potential. The management are suddenly managing shareprice and reverse-engineering

---

[3] In the UK at least, most companies have one or two house brokers who are their primary advisors and the core market makers in the shares.

short-term performance to meet elevated expectations. They are not managing long-term fundamental performance. It is not explicitly wrong. In fact, they are just responding to a perceived expectation and very real institutional pressure. They receive huge external endorsement for this approach. The problem is that the longer term costs of sustaining an excessive short-term premium are very high indeed.

First, there is the direct cash cost to shareholders. Before long almost 10% of the cash raised through share and debt issuance has leaked out of the company to its advisors. This usually equates to the difference between the valuation attached to acquisitions and that attached to the company. In other words, it cancels out the earnings enhancement of the acquisitions which has usually been the justification for the deals. But far more damaging to longer term shareholders is the impact of an unsustainable premium which will eventually deflate due to expectations that cannot be met indefinitely.

Our research would suggest that premiums of greater than 40 to 50% of underlying fundamental value typically endure no more than 2 to 3 years. At that point they suffer a "correction". The moment of correction is usually prompted by a profits warning as the company can no longer deliver on hugely raised expectations for earnings growth. The problem with corrections is that they are unduly punishing on shareholder value. A typical correction involves a reduction in market capitalisation of in excess of 50%. In other words, it is often larger than the premium which preceded it. Over the past 5 years the average correction amongst companies on earnings multiples greater than 30 times has been 50% and

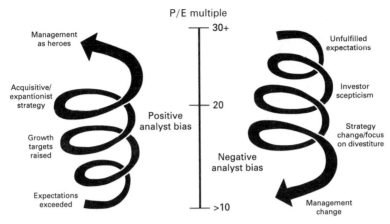

P/E multiple

30+

20

>10

Management
as heroes

Acquisitive/
expantionist
strategy

Growth
targets
raised

Expectations
exceeded

Positive
analyst bias

Negative
analyst bias

Unfulfilled
expectations

Investor
scepticism

Strategy
change/focus
on divestiture

Management
change

Figure 1.1   The cycle of misevaluation

taken 6 months to work its way through the system. To put it another way, during this period of correction the average quoted multiple of this group of highly rated companies has moved from 32 times earnings to around 18. In the correction process the company can often move from being overvalued to being undervalued.

This over-reaction effect becomes particularly pronounced in the 12 months following a downward re-rating. Our research would suggest that it is very hard for an undervalued stock to regain "correct" or fair value. Once a stock has suffered a correction, it takes up to 7 years for it to regain the average market multiple it historically enjoyed before the correction. In other words, the potential under-valuation can be twice as long as the period of overvaluation pre correction. That is a long time in the public markets under general scrutiny and usually too long for even the most loyal value investor. This is clearly painful for all shareholders, whether institutional or individual, unless they have been occupied in the speculative task of gaming the "value trap". But, more importantly, it

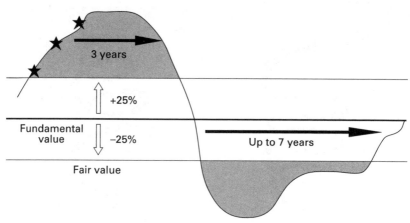

Figure 1.2 An illustrative cycle of misvaluation

represents a real destruction of value for long-term holders of the stock – those for whom fundamentals and longer term TSR have mattered more than short-term shareprice gains.

Just as overvaluation fuels certain management behaviours, so undervaluation also constrains it. Undervaluation tends to create a downward-operating spiral. On a low PE[4] it becomes very hard to justify capital expenditure of any sort. It becomes almost impossible to execute any major corporate development activity. The strategic focus falls on divestiture and a tightening definition of what businesses fall within the realm of core competencies. Whilst this typically boosts cashflow, it also tends to hamper the future growth potential of the business. Any excess cash is either paid out in an enhanced dividend yield or via a share buy-back programme which can give the illusion of success through a one-off boost to the shareprice, but this is usually short-lived.

---

[4] The PE or price earnings ratio is calculated by dividing the shareprice by the forecast full-year earnings per share. It is otherwise known as a company's "rating".

Typically, businesses going through such periods of "work-out" do not make happy places for talented executives to work. Good managers do not want to work for dogs. In effect, the business becomes starved of both investment and talent and, once weakened by starvation, it is very hard to fight back. That is why firms that suffer correction usually subsequently require fundamental change to recover fair value. Typically, this is not just limited to a change of strategy but extends to a change of management. It may even extend to a change of ownership, as the company either gets bought or is broken up. The longer incumbent management hang onto a strategy post a de-rating, the longer it takes for the company to achieve fair value.

In trying to maximise value, management teams of large companies can easily fall into the trap of destroying value. Indeed, a range of academic research confirms common intuition, that the greater the premium achieved by a management team during the upswing, the greater will be the discount post correction.[5] This is the great conundrum that produces so much shareholder and management heartache. In its more recent and extreme form, it has begun to attract serious concern as major companies have faltered, corporate pension funds have fallen into deficit and the institutional fund management industry has gone through a shake-out. At the time of writing this book, large premiums may seem a distant memory for most companies. Almost to a person, the companies interviewed as part of this research felt themselves to be undervalued. In some cases this may be self-deceiving. In others it is a genuine reflection of the boom–bust cycle of the

---

[5] See De Bondt and Thaler (1985).

general misvaluation trap to which large quoted companies are susceptible. However, none of this obviates the obligation on management to use their best endeavours to avoid the misvaluation trap. This book is intended as a plank to achieving that goal.

The road to fair value

So, if maximising shareprice is the wrong objective, what is the right objective? The right objective is to seek to achieve a fair market value for the company. Fair value means that the market capitalisation of the firm accurately reflects its sustainable underlying performance. This has critical implications for how management deal with the markets and run the company. In some cases, this will mean its rating has to fall. In others, it will mean that a mechanism has to be found to re-establish fair value in the eyes of the markets. It implies a very different role for the CEO and demands a different relationship management process with core institutional fund managers.

It also has profound implications for the investment the company makes in beefing up its investor relations function, equipping it with the analytical tools and data sources to conduct fundamental analysis of the company's share register and its market position. It also imposes real challenges on the coordination of a range of corporate actions, through from issues of disclosure, to issues of board composition and investor communications which can only be achieved through close coordination between corporate functions such as strategy, finance and executive management. I call this process "Fair Value Strategy" and this book will focus on the challenge for management of establishing fair value for the company, particularly from a position of undervaluation, and the ongoing process of avoiding the misvaluation trap.

The notion of fair value as the appropriate alternative to value maximisation is not without its detractors. Many hedge fund managers thrive on volatility and benefit from misvaluation, provided they sell out near the top. And other sets of value investors benefit from spotting misvaluation caused by downward overshoots and buying in at the bottom. For this subset of fund managers fair value may appear an irrelevance or even a threat. For the more opportunistic company manager some volatility can also present an opportunity, either pushing the rating as high as possible as quickly as possible before cashing in and moving on or getting involved when the shareprice is undervalued and riding it up. That is how managers make personal fortunes. Given the average tenure of the CEO is less than 3 years, the timing dynamics of the misvaluation cycle is potentially opportune. This book argues that it is the responsibility of the corporate-level manager to optimise performance over the long run and to deliver sustainable returns to shareholders under the assumption that they will hold for greater than 2 years. Fair value is a rejection of gaming.

But before we turn to the principles that underpin the notion of fair value, first we must agree why the markets cannot always be blindly relied upon by management to get it right.

2

Why do the markets get it wrong?

Why do markets fail to identify fair value?

FOR THE PAST FORTY YEARS WE HAVE ALL LIVED WITH THE blithe assumption that markets are "perfect" – that the process of arbitrage between investors trading shares would iron out any temporary misvaluations. If overvaluation exists enough astute investors will "short" the stock and drive it down. If undervalued, the same shrewd investors will spot the opportunity and buy in. The effect amplified across the market as a whole should be that firms are on average correctly valued, and that periods of misvaluation are short and quickly corrected. Given the growth in the number of funds and funds under management, this should make the arbitrage process even more efficient.

The perfect markets argument was first articulated by Milton Friedman and taken firm root ever since. Empirically, it seemed incontrovertible – that provided enough information is available and enough knowledgeable participants engaged, then discrepancies in valuation should quickly be removed through a process of arbitrage. Ten years on, the invention of discounted cashflow analysis and the capital asset pricing model seemed to confirm that there was a clear correlation between a company's net present value based on cashflows and its market value. In other words, stocks are in general correctly valued.

Managerially, this hypothesis is a very comfortable one. It means that the market value of the company will reflect its fundamental value, measured using discounted cashflows. Maybe one or two investors will get it wrong, over- or under-valuing the company for a period of time. But the markets will usually get it right. Assuming perfect markets frees management up from preoccupying themselves with share-holders. What matters for management is ensuring good performance. The markets can be left to get on with their job, and the company with its job. Management need not get diverted into double-guessing the market. In this Utopia, investor relations becomes purely a courtesy exercise and focuses primarily on fulfilling regulatory requirements of disclosure, supported by a modest allocation of senior management time. It was probably this assumption which has meant investor relations is a comparatively underdeveloped function in many large companies whereas corporate strategy has evolved into a sophisticated specialism.

Unfortunately, this blithe assumption is not reality. Markets appear to suffer systematic biases and to promote long periods of misvaluation amongst individual companies. This creates huge demands on management time and energy. It means companies have to manage both stock market performance as well as actual business performance. Far from being able to "leave it to the markets", managers of large companies often wind up investing almost as much time managing the shareprice as they do managing the long-term earnings potential of the business.

There has been no more salutary reminder of market imperfections than the last few years. For the decade starting in the recession of 1990 through to the height of the bull market in 2000, the average P/E multiple for a large UK company rose from a historical average of 17 times earnings to a peak of almost 40 times earnings. The average multiple then plunged, until by late 2002 it was hovering somewhere below its historical average. A not dissimilar story was repeated on the New York Stock Exchange and a far more dramatic one on the tech-rich NASDAQ.

What is most interesting about this exceptionally volatile period is what it exposed about systematic market bias. Those shares which were most highly rated by the markets during the bull run tended to achieve the lowest returns in the subsequent period of correction. Conversely, those that were afforded the lowest rating in the bull period subsequently enjoyed the highest rates of returns post correction. In other words, the markets tended to systematically overvalue and undervalue different groups of stocks during different periods of the overall market cycle (Figure 2.1).[1]

Over a complete cycle of say 10 years, there is some evidence to suggest that these "errors" are indeed corrected. However, given that the average CEO has a 3-year tenure and the

[1] See Alessandri and Bettis (2003).

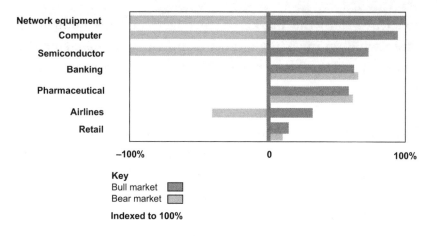

Figure 2.1 Average returns achieved by different quoted sectors in the recent US bull and bear markets.
Source: Adapted from Alessandri and Bettis (2003).

average fund manager 3 years running a particular portfolio, the periods of market "error" are potentially sufficiently long to drive management behaviour which is what we are concerned about in this book.

We can also make some more precise observations about the way these overshoots arise. Research by the behavioural finance fraternity would suggest that the markets make collective decisions about future performance based on sequential data points.[2] The number of data points can be quite small, say between three and five. If a company issues more than three data points suggesting a particular direction of development during a discrete period of time, the markets tend to extrapolate these out into the future. So if, for example, a company issues a series of three trading statements showing marked double-digit growth, the markets

---

[2] See Shleifer (2000).

quickly price in an expectation of double-digit growth into the future. This then drives analysts' discounted cashflow valuations. The same is true with a string of data points indicating a decline. Ongoing decline will be built into the pricing.

The result is potentially systematic bias towards over- and undershooting based on a relatively small data string. In other words, there is a bias towards extreme outcomes. This tallies with the experience of volatility across the markets as a whole and also with the individual experience of companies interviewed as part of this research as they swing from being "in" to being "out" – a highly traumatic transition for management.

But why, given all the information flowing and the number of players, does this happen? The extreme volatility in the recent period is too easily ascribed to the hysterical effect of the dot.com revolution – a moment of madness "never to be repeated". Underlying the "exceptional" irrational exuberance of this latest époque, there is a recurring pattern of behaviour that appears to drive overshoots. Our research would suggest that there are three potential contributing causes:

- The commercial bias of some brokers.

- The evolving bias of some institutional fund managers.

- The behaviour of management themselves.

I will explore each of these potential drivers in turn.

Brokers with a mission

The intermediary market is a complex web of interdependent agents connecting the company with its principal investors (Figure 2.2). What is commonly referred to as the "market system" is, in fact, a network of intermediaries who have grown up to manage the relationship between company and investor. There are only two principles in the market system – the company issuing shares and the investor buying shares. The rest are accounted for by "agents" or advisors which can include certain fund managers themselves who may be working as subcontractors to, for example, pension fund trustees.

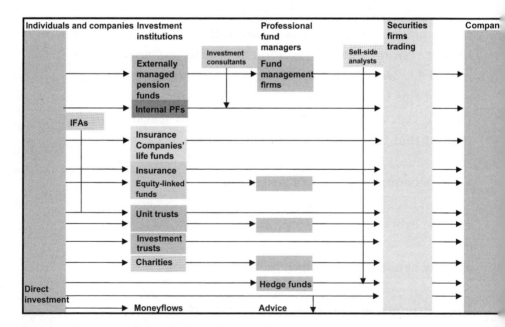

Figure 2.2 Illustration of the market system.
Source: Tony Golding (with thanks).

In effect, the market system is a distribution chain, getting the product, in this case shares, to market. If all the system did was get the product to market as efficiently, objectively and unbiasedly as possible, then this would be quite simple. In other words, if the intermediary web performed a pure logistics function, adding as much value as possible at each step and incurring as little cost. But that is not how things have necessarily evolved. Much of the power in the system is held by the intermediary market of agents and advisors, not by its principals, and these agents can sometimes have distinctly biased agendas that means they are not performing a pure logistics function.

At the heart of the distribution system is the broker. In the UK market, each large quoted company typically appoints one or two "house brokers" as the primary dealers in the firm's stock.[3] Sometimes the house broker is likely to have the best information about which institutions hold the company's stock and which amongst them are likely buyers and sellers. This superior knowledge will partly come from a close knowledge of the company, and also from the fact that, since the company is often paying the broker a retainer fee, it can commit the professional resource to glean this information. The house broker will solicit institutional interest but it will also be the focus of unsolicited interest. If you are a pension fund manager wanting to take a position in the stock, your own broker is likely to turn to the company's house broker to buy the stock as efficiently as possible. Since the house broker will typically employ the lead analyst covering the stock, it

---

[3] In the US market, companies tend not to have the same close ties to a single broker.

will also offer the fullest analyst coverage of the company. The house broker will in effect be the primary market maker in the shares and their direct profit will be generated from commissions on the sale and purchase of stock, combined with the typically small retainer.

A potential problem with the role of the broker as distributor stems from the fact that institutional brokers are not always independent. A robust mid-tier of independent brokers do exist, but they tend to deal with small caps. Brokers catering to larger companies will typically form part of the equities division of an integrated investment bank. There are around 30 major integrated investment banks operating in the City, for example, and the top ten control around 65% of the FTSE 250 accounts and around 80% of the FTSE 100 accounts.

Despite being the original heartland of most UK investment banking operations, the equities divisions of such banks are sometimes not hugely profitable. Average commissions on institutional trades have been driven down relentlessly and retainers average around £100,000 per year against a backdrop of direct staff and data costs to service an account exceeding £200,000 to £300,000 per year. It is not uncommon for up to 50% of the cost base of the equities division to be subsidised by the investment banking division. The investment banker makes his money from commissions on M&A, and capital raising, both equity and the issuance of debt. The reason the investment-banking arm is willing to effectively cross-subsidise the equities division is that the equities group is a primary source of deal flow and market insight for higher ticket investment banking activity, such as rights issues, debt issuance and M&A. Here commission rates are 10 to

20 times higher than in pure equities trading. In some more extreme cases, the equities group can effectively act as the investment bank's marketing department. Post Oxley–Sarbanes few people will openly refer to it as such, and the best banks are building their Chinese Walls as fast as they viably can.

At the core of the equities function is the "sell-side" analyst. The job of analysts is to create objective reports on the company on which institutional fund managers can rely to guide their decision making about the future of the company. The analysts inside the house broker will often have a particularly dominant influence as they will be deemed to have focused insight. The average FTSE company will be covered by around six teams of analysts and on average they will be the subject of around 15 research notes a year. These teams compete for superior ratings from institutional fund managers in annual sector surveys.

Now, these analysts are not cheap. On average they cost their employer around £200,000 a piece. But, of course, the non-house brokers are not charging the client company indirectly for this service. Nor does the securing of house broker status guarantee enough trading commission profit to justify the resource. One traditionally commonplace way of defraying these costs has been to pass them on to the institutional fund manager as part of a "bundled" trading commission. The fund manager in turn passes them back to the principal, whether an insurance company or pension fund. This method of passing back cost is called "softing" and, in the UK at least, is currently under attack from the regulator, as it overtly compromises the transparency of the relationship between broker and fund manager.

But even if "softing" persists, it is not adequate in itself to create a good margin for the broker. That's where the investment bankers come in. If, by virtue of building an intimate relationship with the company, the equities group can directly, or indirectly, help the investment bankers to secure one or two mandates to advise on an acquisition or spin-off, the transaction commission will more than justify the costs of retaining the analysts. The good analyst keeps the bank on close terms with the company to secure advisory mandates, and also positions the bank as the opinion leader in that sector.

What does that mean for the motivation of the analysts? Well, one thing it is difficult to do is openly slate the client company, unless it is truly a dead duck. Between 1997 and 2001 only 3% of analysts' notes carried a sell recommendation. As recently as February 2003, the average UK analyst forecast assumed a growth rate of around 20%. There is some evidence to show that analysts on average tend to over-rate growth stocks and reserve their damnation for a small group of low-growth companies, leading as a result to sustained under-valuation amongst this group. Indeed, this phenomenon has been so pronounced in the United States that average investor returns achieved by US companies appear to negatively correlate to the analyst ratings these companies attract (see Figure 2.3).

It is this overt conflict of interest in the US market that has given rise to the call for the separation of analysis and invest-

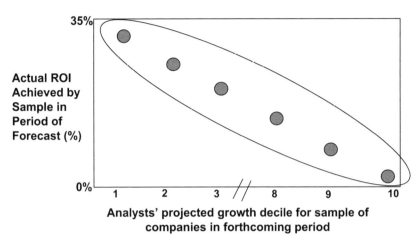

Figure 2.3   The relationship between analyst ratings and investor outcomes. *Source*: Adapted from La Porta (1996).

ment banking enshrined in the Oxley–Sarbanes Act which explicitly presses for the de-coupling of the analyst function and the role of investment banking. Regardless of any potential regulatory pressure, the economic nexus at the core of integrated investment banks would appear to potentially orientate them to driving shareprices higher. A high shareprice means more dealing volume, it means commissions are worth more (a higher base). It also means more deal, cash-raising and advisory fees. As soon as a stock dives then these sources of revenue dry up and the client company loses its attractiveness. The primary motive of the bank, in the form of broker, analyst and investment banker, is logically to drive stock values. Since the average banker, broker and analyst is compensated on an annual bonus basis, their motivation cycle is naturally inclinded to be shorter than that of the fund manager and management.

This is, of course, an intensely simplified picture. The equities groups of banks and analyst functions are populated by many talented and intensely rectitudinous individuals. The frequent complaint of good analysts is in fact that they are constrained by the management of the companies they cover. If they provide too honest a verdict, they will no longer be granted good access. Indeed, their employer may be precluded from lucrative transactions. The observation of the good analyst is often that the management of companies are sometimes more complicit than the banks that cover them. As a result, there has been a steady migration of analytical talent to the "buy-side"[4] where such constraints do not hamper objectivity and good analysis.

So, if everyone knows that this core intermediary group have the potential motive of promoting the share value of client companies, why don't both companies and institutional investors discount their views more energetically? Why isn't the relationship a purely direct one, involving company and buy-side analyst employed by the institutional fund manager directly? Amongst the more battle-hardened management teams, there appears to be a rumbling debate about cutting out the house broker altogether and building up in-house expertise, a notion I will touch on in more detail presently.

In these debates, the issue is typically raised of whom the broker is working for in the first place. The lifeblood of the broker is the relationship with the community of in-stitutional fund managers who create commissions and potentially defray the operating costs of brokers. How does this marry with the fact that they are retained by companies

---

[4] The term "buy-side" refers to the fund managers whereas the "sell-side" refers to the broker.

as brokers? When push comes to shove, many brokers will inevitably tend to follow the interests of the fund manager and not those of the company. There are, after all, infinite ways to invest someone else's money and it is the money that generates the commission.

Yet, despite the internal rumblings, no large companies in the UK have ditched their house broker relationship. Thirty years of dependence on a series of house brokers have effectively distanced many companies away from knowledge of the investor market. This appears to produce a sensation in many we spoke to as part of this research that they cannot afford to alienate their primary broker. "If we went round them, and reduced their fees, they wouldn't put our stock in front of their best relationships. We'd be marginalised." It is surprising how much power house brokers are attributed with having. This is even more surprising if you think of the relationship of the company with its core investors. Many of the core investors of larger companies will be well known to the management. Some may have held the stock for a year or even several years. Certainly, the CEO will have met the key fund managers on a number of occasions. You might think therefore that the broker would have no role. Far from it. Reliance on the broker is often ingrained.

It is clear from our research that most companies invest comparatively little direct specialist resource in managing the relationship with institutional investors. They are likely to operate an investor relations function with two or three people, most of whose time will be consumed with the mammoth logistics exercise of preparing presentational material and organising the mechanics of around 60 investor meetings a year, an AGM, an interim results presentation, plus a set of analysts' updates. In addition, the Investor Relations (IR) folk will have responsibility for producing the annual report and responding to an endless stream of enquiries, mostly from non-core analysts and retail investors. For this reason, the level of strategic thinking championed by the IR group is not always as deep as it should be. The access to information about investor behaviour also tends to be limited. There is often little systematic analysis of the shareholder register. Knowledge about particular fund managers tends to be personalised and anecdotal. The house broker fills this void, able to invest in information systems and analytical resource.

You might also expect fund managers to basically disregard the output of the sell-side analyst, binning research notes much like any direct mail shot. Yet, that is not how things work in practice. Lead sell-side analysts' notes are read by fund managers and a good analyst has the power to influence investor opinion quite dramatically. In the recent banking downturn, most investment banks have hung onto their well-rated analysts despite the increasing limitations put on cross-referral. There is clear recognition that superior knowledge is key to competitive advantage, even if the process of monetising it is no longer so clear and even if fund managers can no longer pass the costs of this insight from the broker onto their ultimate client in an opaque fashion. Whilst the analyst function will in all likelihood shrink and migrate from the sell-side to the buy-side, the good broker will fight to retain that edge.

The important point is that it is not legitimate for management to lay the blame for misvaluation at the analysts' feet.

Most companies are complicit in situations of overvaluation. Around 80% of an analysts' notes are seen by the company before they are released, putting the company in a position to influence them, which they typically do. Analysts' notes tend to be viewed by management as a way of communicating forecasts indirectly. Indeed, well-rated analysts will often complain about the level of company interference, particularly when analysis reveals a valuation problem. Conversely, few managers will challenge a premium and most tend to be happy with optimistic forecasts.

How should companies seeking fair value respond to this situation? Ignore the sell-side analyst community altogether, in the way that companies such as Gillette and HP have proposed? Should they show increasing reluctance to give guidance to analysts on forecasts which will effectively undermine the advantage held by the house analyst? Should they reduce access to the management team? Should they send the signal that they are no longer willing to divert strategy to short-term earnings demands? This might sound principled and strong but, on the whole, none of these responses are practicable.

The system has to be managed, not short-circuited. It is also too easy to write off the contribution of the good sell-side analyst and the good broker. The best analysts remain very influential amongst under-resourced fund managers and highly impactful on short-term stock prices. The best brokers have a deep understanding of the behaviour of fund managers. The broker and analyst nexus can have an impact on sustaining misvaluation but it is a channel that cannot be ignored or bypassed. Instead, it has to be integrated by management into delivering a fair value strategy.

The rise of the passive investor

What about the institutional fund manager in this process? As principals with abundant information, surely they are in a position to bring sanity to the market? Given there are over 7,000 individual fund managers with holdings in UK equities, there are surely enough to create a perfect market? Any mis-valuation will be immediately spotted and ironed out through natural arbitrage? It appears that is not how things always work.

Around 70% of institutional money is farmed out to special-ist fund management businesses rather than being managed in-house (we will explore the precise nature and composition of institutional investors in Chapter 3). As a general rule, pension trustees favour subcontracting out management and insurance funds favour in-house management. In either case, there will be a professional manager charged with achieving target returns against key benchmark indices and peer group funds. The primary motive of the fund manager is to out-perform against the leading index and their peer funds. In the case of the UK manager this means the FTSE All Share Actuarial Index, and against their fund management peer competition, both of which will be specified in the mandate from the principals and their advisors.

Professional fund managers are, in principle, in an excellent position to scrutinise and analyse all the available data. They increasingly tend to employ their own dedicated analysts whose cost is spread across a number of portfolios. As we have discussed, often they will also draw on the information-gathering resources of the brokers with whom they place trades and then pass this cost on. This effectively means they can source as much market information as they want at comparatively low direct cost. What could be a better position to be in from which to beat the markets?

In practice, however, this is not how all large-cap fund managers behave. Our research would suggest that many large-cap fund managers tend to act indirectly to reinforce general market momentum rather than buck it. That may sound like a pretty strange statement. After all, institutional fund managers are very smart characters. They are entirely au fait with the sell-side analyst game. They know the forecasts are bullish, that the growth expectations can be unrealistic. They even employ buy-side analysts who ostensibly have no such vested interest other than finding the truth. So, why do they go along with the bias of the intermediary machine? Some don't. Some see the pitfalls and quickly become sellers of growth stocks into a rising market and buyers where there is real value. But many large-cap fund managers appear to adopt a far more passive approach, closely hugging the index and the pack. This would on the face of it appear entirely counter-logical. Surely an astute manager would sell when there is a clear premium and buy on a discount? But, that is not how many large-cap funds appear to behave in practice.

The decision to deviate far from the index is a momentous one unless a fund manager feels with some certainty they can significantly outperform the index and their peer group as a result. If they resist the momentum of the market and dump rising stocks aggressively, the cost in terms of relative performance could jeopardise their mandate. Their job is made far easier and less risky in a rising, premium-driven market. In a bear market index-based strategies, unless specifically mandated by the trustees, look far less viable and many funds, unused to anything but a passive approach, come unstuck. But, the fact is that around 20% of large-cap funds are specifically mandated by their institutional trustees to adopt a passive approach and another 25–30% have a closet index mandate which awards them some weighting discretion but within close parameters centred on the index.

For reasons that we will explore in Chapter 3, our research suggests that of the remaining 50% of large-cap funds under management, the majority are effectively weighted at or close to the index. The net effect is that active fund management constitutes only a small proportion of the whole and much of this is dominated by hedge funds and overseas funds whose fundamental interest in the company may be low.

The potentially distorting effect of index-related behaviour is that it links investment decisions to market movements and not to company fundamentals. An index-driven fund manager will trade in and out as a company or sector loses or gains weight relative to the index, but without direct reference to its fundamentals. The asset management process becomes one about shareprice, and not fundamental asset value. This appears to hold true even in situations of blatant misvaluation and in particular with large premiums. Whilst many fund managers may see the error in a prevailing market valuation, many will also be nervous about taking a stand and selling or buying differentially from the pack. They have a lot to lose by being the martyr. If the index continues to climb and they are not part of the herd movement, their relative performance will be poor. If they stay in and the index falls, their relative performance may still be acceptable. As a result, there appears to be the basis for a strong, systemic bias in favour of holding premium stocks and ignoring discounted stocks. The bias of analysts reinforces this dynamic.

There are, of course, those large-cap fund managers who are both active and target value. But, in reality this group probably comprises no more than around 5% to 10% of funds under management in the UK, for example. They happen to be the most important 5% to 10% as we will see.

So, why does a clever, insightful, ambitious fund manager follow this passive path even when their mandate does not demand it? One possible explanation is that many fund managers are constrained by the size of their task. A typical individual large-cap fund manager oversees eight portfolios, each containing around 85 stocks. This makes opportunities for fundamental research limited. As fund management companies come under pressure to cut costs and increase the "leverage" of their good managers, presumably the amount of time any fund manager can dedicate to fundamental insight on particular companies is declining rather than increasing. The likely decline in softing may reduce their willingness to undertake fundamental research. As fund managers consolidate and trustees, faced with mounting fiduciary responsibilities, get more conservative, there are no real grounds to suppose that indexation will do anything but strengthen its grip.

The passive investor poses a real challenge for company management. If a fund holds shares as part of an index portfolio, they are unlikely to reveal the nature of their mandate to management. As a result, the company may expend a large amount of senior resource trying to influence them, when in reality the fund manager has no intrinsic interest in the company's strategy. The result is frustration, wasted energy and misunderstanding – a set of outcomes that our research suggest is not hugely uncommon.

We know that shareprice movements are set at the margin by directional traders in, say, 2–3% of the company's shares. The challenge for management becomes the task of identifying that small number of fund managers (our research suggests that at any point in time this may be only 2 or 3 out of a total register of 30 to 40) who are setting the price and getting the herd moving. This is a real challenge and I dedicate a chapter to working out how to do this (Chapter 6). It is essential that companies do this because it is herd movements that cause the price to overshoot, and once herds are set in motion they are impossible to stop.

Sipping from the poisoned chalice

So, where does responsibility ultimately fall for such market imperfections and the damage they can cause? Can management innocently point to an innately flawed system and absolve themselves? The reality is that management is usually to some degree complicit in the process of overshoots. In the boom period till mid-2000, there was scant little remark from major CEOs that they felt a near doubling of valuation parameters from 1995 was perhaps "over-egging" it. The intermediary market was energetic in sustaining high ratings that allowed deals to be done on an earnings-enhancing basis, boosting earnings per share and apparently creating value for the company. But there was no suggestion that the double-digit growth implied in most valuations was unsustainable. Indeed, most companies were explicitly managed for high growth, particularly through acquisition. Most CEOs actively geared their strategies to fulfil these growth expectations. The explosion of deal activity on the back of inflated multiples in the public markets made it easier for most corporates to acquire smaller companies and private businesses at valuations sufficiently discounted v. their own that they could achieve high rates of earnings per share (EPS) growth. Hence, they could persuade everyone, including themselves, that they could deliver the growth implicit in their own market valuations. Management were complicit in corroborating forecasts of growth which tied them to aggressive acquisition schedules. Even fund managers who should have known better were often supportive of deal activity to sustain growth.

Through a process of external prompting (often from unlikely quarters such as academics) and the urgings of self-interest, management incentives became umbilically linked to total shareholder returns and hence shareprice. By 2000, a majority of average director compensation was being met in the form of stock options or shareprice-related performance bonuses.

These typically divided into short-term incentive plans (STIPs) that paid out annually and long-term plans (LTIPs) that paid out between 3 and 5 years, almost exclusively in shares or options. The philosophy of linking total shareholder return (TSR) and compensation was driven deep into the bedrock of many organisations. The dominant technique used to do this was the tenet of value based management or VBM.

VBM has at one point or another been adopted by around half of all FTSE and Fortune 500 companies, to a lesser or greater extent (although many have now dropped it). Its principle proposition was to link the most desegregated but measurable management actions (or value drivers) back up directly to shareholder outcomes, usually through a measurement cascade (see Figure 2.4). In essence, it proposed that rather than just board-level executives being incentivised in shares and tied to share performance, the same logic could be extended to all levels of management.

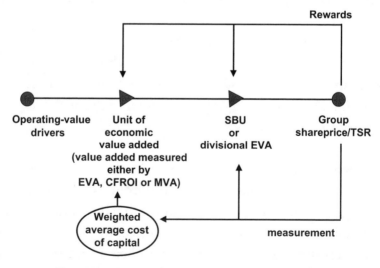

Figure 2.4 A typical VBM measurement cascade.

In times of rising shareprices, this logic seemed to work admirably. Increased productivity and effectiveness at a grass roots level would be reflected in greater profitability and higher TSR. Managers deep inside the company could appear to contribute directly to driving the value of their shares and to benefit from the rewards of doing so. In this buoyant environment, hard efforts appeared to be swiftly rewarded and the VBM process met with wide endorsement as an empowering tool. High ratings, and indeed overvaluation, simply added fizz to this heady cocktail. At Enron even secretaries were paper millionaires.

However, with a general decline in shareprices, the positive reinforcement effect of the VBM system quickly became undermined. Companies found their shareprice-based incentive schemes completely out of sync with the needs of the organisation. Hard efforts to improve productivity were often met with shareprice falls. Options disappeared underwater by the stack. As a result, many companies reverted to traditional measures of internal profitability rather than using proxies for shareprice. But there can be little doubt that VBM made its own contribution to the acceleration of growth expectations and premiums. Management have to shoulder their share of the blame in stoking market misvaluation.

The cost of market imperfections

The days of large premiums may now seem distant to many companies. As soon as stock values began to decline in late 2000, the cracks in many company's growth stories opened up. The relatively anaemic growth potential of many large businesses in relatively mature markets was exposed as soon as transactional flow slowed. As multiples fell, so large companies could no longer acquire bascd on valuation arbitrage, and those companies they had acquired on this basis often began to themselves falter, failing to produce promised "synergies". The result was compounded slower growth, with the appearance of rapid deceleration even if the fundamental growth of core businesses remained quite respectable and, at the time of writing this book, has now picked up again in general. Lowered shareprices have in many cases precipitated fundamental changes in strategy and management.

This has, of course, exposed the nature of the flipside of misvaluation – the characteristic overshoot on the downside. The problem with negative market sentiment is that the markets appear to have a strong bias against lowly rated companies, in precisely the same way they have a bias in favour of highly rated companies. The result, following an episode of downward re-rating, can often be undervaluation. Periods of undervaluation typically follow those of steep premiums, except they are different in character and impact. Premiums rarely last more than 3 years and can be large, often exceeding 50%. When they are lost they are lost quickly. Discounts will typically be at least as deep but more importantly they appear to endure far longer. For a company that has moved into material discount it typically takes up to 7 years to regain fair value. This will probably entail major structural change, such as change of control or break-up. Our research suggests that around half of the companies that fall into deep discount will suffer structural change.

The cost for all remaining stakeholders of undervaluation is high indeed, although many, including fund managers, brokers and even management, may have got out in the meantime. An undervalued company is typically compelled to stop all major corporate activity, and particularly acquisitions which institutional shareholders will no longer support. As a result, the fee-earning opportunities for bankers and other intermediaries collapses – trade volumes decline, debt issuance falls and the equity opportunities dry up. Consequently, the number of analysts following the stock declines, and the ability of management to attract their attention dwindles, even if there is a perceived value opportunity. The economic motive for the intermediary system to support the company falls away.

This exaggerated deceleration is compounded by the nature of the average large-cap institutional investor base. Because the company will have declined as part of the index, or indeed exited key indices altogether, the bulk of index-led investors will sell accordingly. Typically, their exit will not occur in line with fair value, but reflect the re-weighting of the company in the index. The result is an accelerated downward pressure on the shareprice and a self-fulfilling prophecy of undervaluation. The company, and particularly its management, will suddenly feel intensely vulnerable.

Not surprisingly, the reaction from more active investors to situations of undervaluation is to seek to change the management, realising that the markets are biased against them and that it will typically require a fundamental trigger to alter perceptions by fellow active investors. The evidence is now becoming clearer that changing management is not the silver bullet it is sometimes assumed to be. Our research suggests that new management in its own right does not reliably result in a sustainable uplift in value, even if it can produce an immediate up-tick. Addressing undervaluation usually requires more systemic changes. Above all, seeking to recover fair value is a long-term campaign, averaging a number of years. It requires recognition and management of the biases of the environment in which the company is operating.

It is abundantly clear that the best course for a company is to espouse a strategy of fair value before misvaluation establishes itself in the first place. Unless a company is managed for fair value, it is likely to wind up misvalued, and misvaluation carries a high cost. But, where does management start on the fair value road? As with all markets, the best place to start is understanding the customer, in this case the institutional fund manager. That's where we go next.

3

Understanding the institutional fund manager

Why do fund managers behave as they do and what can management do about it?

AVOIDING THE PITFALLS OF OVERSHOOTS DEMANDS THAT a company has a thorough understanding of its institutional investor base. The shareholder register holds the key to the shareprice, the same way as the customer list holds the potential for insight into revenue. That makes it deserving of huge attention and analysis by management – something that appears not to be invested in sufficiently by many companies.

I have already talked about the limitations of relying unquestioningly on the house broker as the sole champion of investor analysis and insight. Our research suggests that many companies do not subject movements in the register to regular, systematic analysis to understand who is driving the shareprice. Often they lack the resources to follow proxy trades through to their underlying principals and aggregate such trades into an overall picture. They also do not always attempt to determine who is actually driving the price rather than passively following the herd. Insight into important trading movements is too often based on single data points, feel and tip-offs from the broker. The objective of this book is to change that approach and to encourage management to focus resources on those investors that matter, deepening the company's understanding of them in the process in co-operation with the broker.

The retail punter

In focusing attention, the first tranche of the register that can be treated separately is that represented by the retail investor. In the UK, institutional investors typically account for between 70% and 90% by value of the register of any large-cap company. The balance is accounted for by retail investors. In the US, the retail investor holds roughly double that amount. There has been much talk of the alleged increasing importance of the retail trader to the fate of the company shareprice. The Internet has given power to the day trader; information is readily available in a way it never was 10 years ago; the retail brokerage industry has expanded quickly; and the level of familiarity with shares has expanded enormously. But, the influence of the retail investor is usually exaggerated.

A large-cap stock may have 10,000 private individuals holding its stock, on average accounting for less than 15% of the equity between them. Individually, they have the right to attend AGMs and quite often they will barrage the Investor Relations (IR) director with enquiries, consuming plenty of senior management resource in the process. In theory, they can stir things up. But, in practice, they rarely do. Most AGMs are anticlimactic little affairs attended by a few individuals and the company's advisors. More importantly, retail holders rarely ever act proactively in tandem. That is to say, their activity rarely initiates a major movement in the stock. With the exception of some of the larger private client brokers, this is the role of the institutional fund manager.

The institutional fund manager typically tries to hold less than 3% of the stock of any individual company to escape the need to disclose their holding, and even then they may hold shares through a proxy or divide their holdings across multiple sub-funds. Most large-cap registers are accounted for by around 30–40 institutional investors, with perhaps 4 or 5 weighing in above the disclosure threshold. In this institutionally dominated world, the retail investor can only provide momentum to institutional trades, exaggerating underlying price movements. In the case of medium- and small-cap stocks the mix will be different and management will typically have a larger stake, along with other wealthy individuals. In these circumstances their individual trades may have as dramatic an effect on shareprice as institutional trades. But, one clear indicator that a company has graduated from small to mid cap or large cap is that the register shifts decisively towards institutional holders of the stock.

Knowing the protagonists

Institutional fund managers are complex characters for a business manager to get his or her hands around. Whilst some are well known, their strategies well stated, and their proclivities established, others are completely opaque. It may even be difficult to work out who they are if they trade through proxies. Even if a particular fund is a known quantity, the strategy of the individual fund manager may be far less predictable. The average length of employment of a fund manager on a particular portfolio is 3 years, slightly longer than the average fund mandate, and each new manager typically introduces a new strategy to the portfolio they inherit. This means that what started out looking like a simple task of tracking the activity of 30 shareholders is in fact a major task of detective work, particularly so as the average holding period of an individual stock has fallen from 3 years to less than 2 years. Understanding the motives of each fund manager and predicting their behaviour is a real skill that few companies have fully honed.

The foremost protagonists in the institutional fund game are the pension funds, the insurance funds, the investment funds and overseas investors. Between them, these four groups account for around 75% of equity holdings. The less significant amongst this group are the investment funds which account for less than 10% of institutional holdings. Investment funds are themselves quoted and primarily act as vehicles for wealthy investors. The real game lies with the pension funds, the insurance funds and, increasingly, foreign funds and also the new breed of hedge funds.

At a very generic level, a number of commentators have made much hay out of trying to draw generic distinctions between these types of investors, implying that this can lend insight into their behaviour. Pension and insurance funds do tend to have some generic differences. Pension funds have classically been longer term holders of stock, not favouring churn in their portfolios. This makes sense because the liabilities they are investing to meet are also long term in nature. Investment funds, by contrast, have tended to be much more active traders of their portfolios. Insurance funds have classically favoured more active management whereas pension funds have tended towards an index bias. They have also adopted different approaches towards investment procedures. Insurance funds, for a variety of reasons, early on evolved their own in-house fund management capability. Over the years this strategy has been reinforced, with the result that up to 90% of insurance cash is invested using in-house managers. By contrast, around 90% of pension fund cash is farmed out to specialist external fund managers, often controlled by insurance funds. It is hard to know how, given the relative underperformance by some of these independent managers over the past 5 years, this subcontraction process will evolve.

This distinction may account for certain possible differences in investment approach between pension and insurance cash. The executives of insurance companies responsible for allocating assets to fund managers may benefit from senior fund management allocation experience. They will have familiarity with the effectiveness of different performance terms, and how to respond to different performance outcomes. For the trustee of a pension fund, typically relatively modestly paid for the role and potentially unversed in the details of investment procedure, life may be very different. In the absence of personal experience they typically have to call on external expertise. The allocation process of pension money to external fund management companies is typically overseen by Investment Consultants who advise trustees on the choice of manager and investment strategy.

Whilst these distinctions do imply potential differences in investment style between pension and insurance money, it is not a sound basis on which management can draw conclusions about the likely behaviour of different fund managers. Just because a manager overseas pension money does not mean they are likely to be a longer term holder or more index-oriented than another fund manager with insurance assets. Such basic segmentation does not appear to work.

What is clear is that the number of institutional asset holders is set to continue to shrink. In the insurance sector six players control 86% of insurance assets. Similarly, seven pension fund companies account for around 70% of pension assets. The effect of consolidating institutions has been to produce pronounced concentration amongst fund managers. The top eight fund management companies account for 65% of funds under management and control around 40% of the overall listed market for stocks in the UK. That is an extraordinary level of concentration for such a large market.

One by-product of this is that an increasing amount of institutional money is now pooled rather than being run individually. This means that the distinction between pension and insurance cash will decline even further. It also means the amount of time individual fund managers have to spend on fundamental research is likely to fall. A by-product of consolidation is the increasingly conservative nature of the investment decision itself by the fund manager, as scale and tight performance parameters continue to promote the cause of indexation.

An important contributor to increased conservatism amongst all fund managers is the role of the investment consultant. There are eight significant investment consultancy groups of whom the most well known are probably Bacon and Woodrow. Investment consultants have a very strong influence on the allocation decision by pension trustees and on shaping the investment strategy of the fund manager, including some insurance-controlled fund managers, through the mandate. Most investment consultants favour larger, well-established fund management companies with strategies that minimise "dispersion" from the index. Their big fear is being faced with major underperformance as a result of one of their recommendations. As a result, they tend to channel mandates to a small coterie of larger fund management companies, themselves with conservative, low-dispersion strategies.

This focus on a handful of suppliers also makes good economic sense for the advisor. The average fee for an advisor on a major placement is around £300,000, which is comparatively small in proportion to the funds being placed. As a result, the incentive to make an (easy) choice and place the funds into known hands is very strong indeed. This has probably been a significant driver of the consolidation of the fund management industry. The recently poor performance of a section of the fund management industry at the time of writing this book, 40% of whom had failed to even reach the index, will almost certainly prompt further consolidation.

The challenges of conservatism

This has all produced some distinct characteristics amongst some large institutional shareholders which are more important than generic distinctions between assets in terms of understanding investor behaviour. First, the fund manager is usually distinct from the ultimate owner of the assets, and the framework under which they are given direction to manage those assets will impose tight restrictions (perceived or real) on their decision making. The fund manager typically manages the money under a mandate of 2 years' duration, less than the life-span of the typical strategic planning cycle of the companies in which they invest. The mandate will specify the benchmark index against which the fund is being measured and the peer group of funds it is expected to match. It will be required to beat the index after fully loaded fees as well as achieve a respectable performance relative to its peers typically expressed in quartiles (e.g., top-quartile performance, etc.). These rules will condition the core behaviour of fund managers as it will flow through to their own compensation.

Second, there is the old complaint about short-termism. Given the short mandate lifetime, it is possible that the individual fund manager will not be concerned with the long-term view. The fact that a company's strategy may deliver in 5 years may be irrelevant compared with annual performance. This time horizon is ultimately down to the mandate and asset owner, whether pension or insurance fund. For the fund manager, short time horizons are in fact a major headache. Trading positions costs money in terms of commissions and also tax and hence these costs reduce average returns. Trading also demands time and attention – something fund managers have very little to spare. So, the fund manager is not ultimately to blame. Their hands are tied by the mandate.

Third, there is a very practical pressure on the fund manager. In order to reduce costs, and hence the barrier to at least meeting the index, most fund management companies are increasing the number of portfolios managed by individual fund managers. The average large-cap fund manager now oversees six to eight portfolios, each containing around 85 different shares. This again impacts the time they have free to dedicate to analysing individual stocks. On average, a couple of annual meetings with each management team in their portfolio is all they can spare.

These by-products of the mandate process, combined with increasingly conservative mandate principles, begins to explain the rise of indexation, the ultimate expression of conservative professional investing. Up to 50% of the average large quoted company's share register will probably be in the hands of explicit tracker or closet index funds. The challenge for the company of index and closet index funds is their managers may not really care about the company *per se*. Their only interest is whether the company is included in an index or not and how it is weighted. It is because of the power of this traction that when a company ascends into a major index its shares usually appreciate by around 3% on the day of announcement. When it leaves an index the shares typically fall by around 15% during the prolonged exit period. Since indexes are driven by market capitalisation, they directly reflect shareprice and tend to increase the pressure on management to perform very predictably within tight parameters.

The main challenge of indexers for management is that they are easily mistaken for active traders. At one end of the indexer spectrum are those funds that obviously and explicitly espouse a major index, such as the FTSE Actuarial All Share Index. Then further along the spectrum are a range of more exotic indexes specified in certain mandates. Beyond this 15% or so of funds, indexers get far harder to identify and it is far less clear to an external observer whether the fund has an index mandate or not. A fund may operate under an amalgam of sectoral indexes or indeed a house index. At these points on the spectrum, funds are easily mistaken for active traders, and a large amount of management energy can be spent trying to woo them when the criteria for their position is not directly related to intrinsic performance of the company. If they persistently fail to attend any analyst meetings, never make calls to the IR director, and express no interest in meeting management, that may be a reasonable give-away. However, fund managers are understandably reluctant to betray their investment strategies to investee companies, and their observations in meetings are easily misinterpreted.

An added challenge for management comes from the fact that, even where there is not an explicit index requirement in the mandate, large-cap fund managers are increasingly managing their supposedly "active" funds largely in line with the index. These are called closet indexers and probably comprise a further 25% of funds under management, bringing the

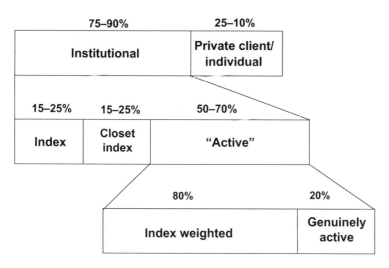

Figure 3.1 Profile of the institutional investor market.

pretty-much-straight index brigade to around half of funds under management.

The really interesting finding of our research was that, of the remaining half of large-cap funds that are supposedly highly actively managed, up to 80% of these may closely follow the index weighting, although no firm numbers are available on this (see Figure 3.1). One possible explanation would appear to lie with the motivation of the individual fund manager. The pressure on the individual fund manager not to underperform the index and the peer group is intense. The cost of failure appears to be perceived as far higher than the cost of delivering what amounts to pedestrian perform-ance of around average index returns. The cost of falling outside the peer group also appears to outweigh the perceived benefit of trying to beat it. The fund manager may get a bonus for outperformance but the cost of underperformance is terminal.

It seems likely from our research that the average large-cap fund manager will be given increasingly less discretion over major weighting decisions, as decisions on key sectors and stocks are increasingly made by senior fund managers across an entire set of portfolios within a fund management company. The remorseless concentration of both stocks and sectors within major indexes makes this logic ever more compelling. It also enables fund management groups to lower costs in the process. In the UK, for example, seven stocks account for nearly 40% of the FTSE and four sectors for 50% of total market capitalisation. For example, the decision whether or not to weight in line with the market for Vodafone alone may account for 5% of a portfolio. This leaves only marginal fund capacity which is genuinely actively traded on the basis of individual company insight at grass roots level.

The quest for culprits

Logically, index-based funds will not tend to give the market initial direction, but they will give it huge momentum. So, in a tracker-dominated world, who provides direction? The first tier of potential culprits are the active institutional funds. They tend to be small compared with their index-oriented brethren. An active fund might only have £100m of assets under management. But, they pack a punch far bigger than their weight. Shareprices tend to be set at the margin and active trading of shares may well produce a shareprice reaction of an order of magnitude to those trades. Two per cent of shares traded may well create more than a 10% shift in price,

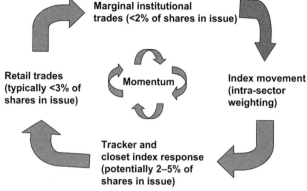

Figure 3.2 The momentum effect of indexation.

as Rentokil discovered when it came off its 20% growth trajectory and suffered a 20% fall in value based on less than 2% of its shares being traded. This is partly explained by the momentum effect as indexers of one variety or another follow small shifts in weighting, followed by retail investors. In a less than liquid stock small trades can produce large movements in their own right (Figure 3.2).

Often these active funds may sit within much larger passive fund families as value leaders to allure institutional trustees to the company. The number of stocks in their portfolios will tend to be lower than in an index fund and their involvement with the companies far greater, and potentially very positive.

Beyond the plain vanilla, active, institutional fund managers, there are a more exotic cadre of professional investors who are the ones often attributed with actually driving market direction. Amongst this spicy blend are the hedge funds, the "active value" funds, the vulture funds, the arbitrageurs, to name but a few. Their investment patterns and strategies are very different from the primary institutional fund managers. Most of them are primarily interested in the anomalous movements in the market for stocks which can temporarily be exploited to their gain. Broadly speaking, such funds thrive on volatility and pricing disruption. They often base at least part of their strategy on the use of derivatives which minimise their capital commitment to the underlying shares, and in turn accentuate pre-existing volatility. Unlike mainstream institutional funds, they also tend to operate internationally, typically across the UK and US markets.

Over the last 10 years these types of funds have proliferated, numbering perhaps tens of thousands globally, as institutions have increased their allocation to "alternative public asset classes" from around 2% of funds under management to around 8%, roughly in line with the growth in private equity fund allocation. They are secretive, disclosing little information. As they operate globally across borders, often it is quite hard to work out where the key decision makers are actually based. They are usually particularly frustrating for management to deal with. They may be based in Bermuda, operate through proxy holdings and in all probability they will not want to debate the finer points of strategy with management. They may not even hold any underlying shares but rather operate through options or other derivatives.

Even in the case of the more identifiable funds in this class, the company will typically not know the name of the fund manager and the fund manager will have little interest in making contact with the company. Like the index funds, they are very hard to manage in any conventional sense. But, unlike the index funds, their behaviour can and often does lead to major price movements. Indeed, their strategy is often explicitly to force violent price movements from which to capitalise. They also indirectly interact with more stable investors by borrowing stock or selling it short.

Embedded in this group are the value investors whose mission is to hone onto undervalued companies and sectors based on fundamental research. These fund managers clearly take a keen interest in strategy and, indeed, will probably have an interest that is clearly aligned to that of long-term holders of the stock. But, as a subset of this more exotic cadre of active fund managers they are relatively rare beasts. Often they can also create an uncomfortable ride for management, as I will come onto presently.

Finally, there is yet another ingredient to disrupt the illusion of a stable, comprehensible universe of fund managers – the overseas investor. Foreign funds have grown from around 5% of total market capitalisation in 1992 to up to around 10% today, although the exact number is not known. The fund managers of foreign funds tend to be a different breed to their UK counterparts. For a start, they tend to be less index-based and more active in their investment strategies. But, this positive quality from management's standpoint (e.g., an active investor is in principle concerned with strategy and management quality) is matched by unattractive qualities. It tends to be harder for management to get a firm grip on the fund's strategy and to predict its behaviour, and it is more difficult for the CEO and CFO to manage the relationship with them in their traditional City style of regular chats, lunches and collegial gatherings. In other words it is a more objective, dispassionate relationship which is typically uncomfortable for established management teams. Like the hedge funds, overseas funds are often perceived to be a potential threat.

In a world of indexers, it is by definition the trading pattern of this active minority that sets the price. In fact, our research suggests that it is usually the trading activity of only two to three active investors in a particular company that initiates a major movement in price which then becomes exaggerated by subsequent index shifts. It is not uncommon for these investors to hold fairly small blocks of shares – perhaps 0.5% of the share capital – but through their trading of such blocks they significantly move the price.

Often these active investors will in turn be actively watched by other more passive fund managers who look for the lead in share movements, again compounding the effect of their decision making. This can come down to pretty basic behaviours. At analysts' meetings, people in the room will often know who is the active investor in a particular company and they will look for signs of how they might be about to act – difficult questions, negative expressions, excessive note taking. The herd is always looking for the leader who they believe knows more than they do.

The frustrating thing for management is that, even if they can identify these funds (which in itself is a big challenge we will come to in detail in Chapter 6), the fund manager in question may be pursuing a strategy that bears no relationship to the company's long-term performance. Like the indexers, they may present a deaf set of ears. The hedge fund, using derivatives, may be shorting the stock as part of an interest-rate hedge. They won't return calls. They may only be in the stock for a month. But, as directionally active traders they will influence the price.

The company view

Most companies characterise institutional investors on two dimensions – that of size and that of location. Management teams quite naturally tend to prioritise the attention given to fund managers according to their holdings – whether they have more than 3%, more than 1% and lastly less than 1%. This will broadly determine the number of meetings the CEO and CFO will have with each fund manager. Typically, foreign funds will receive half the attention of national domestic funds, with management conducting a single foreign road show in each major market once a year.

But, are size and location the ultimate determinants of the importance of investors to the company? It is clear the company would be unwise to ignore large investors. But, beyond that, it should be equally clear from the observations so far that just because a fund manager holds a material block of stock, it does not mean that they necessarily have any keen interest in fundamental, long-term performance or strategy. If their holding reflects a sectoral index strategy or, if they hold a large derivative position, they may have little long-term commitment. Management attention may be largely mis-spent on them and with it the most valuable resource at the company's disposal.

The phrase management often use to distinguish between types of institutional investor is "loyal" v. "unloyal", meaning those funds who are apparently at least long-term holders as opposed to those that trade in and out. The "loyalist" institutional holders of the stock are logically attributed with underpinning the long-term shareprice. Their tolerance to shareprice movement will presumably be more robust. They may not, for example, trade out of the stock because of a 10% fall in shareprice. It is often observed that the initial investment of such funds will have been made on value, not growth grounds. The weighting of the particular stock in their portfolio may also tend to be more significant, commanding a higher proportion of their attention. It is logically interpreted that loyalists tend to be more concerned with strategy and "management quality" than short-term earnings. Disloyal investors are, by contrast, simply concerned with the short-term uplift.

The logic supporting the notion of shareholder loyalty makes some intuitive sense from the fund manager's perspective. If you are a fund manager balancing five portfolios of a hundred stocks each, it is far easier if you can rely on being a long-term holder of a number of core stocks. There will have been a cost to entry, and there will be a similar cost to exit, which will dent fund performance. If there is a long-term capital gain, there is also the thorny issue of tax. Selling off large positions also usually depresses the average share value during the exit process as the fund sells down the offer curve. It is entirely rational that fund managers should prefer to hold rather than trade.

Most senior managers would deeply resent any suggestion that they could possibly fail to identify who are their loyalist holders v. disloyal holders. On average, the CEO and CFO will meet with larger shareholders two or three times a year and they may have a number of additional contacts over the phone or via email. They are likely to feel they are "closely in touch". Senior managers often convince themselves that their knowledge of their core investors is sufficient to make their judgement about possible moves as good as it could hope to be. Analysis is perceived as unnecessary and too clumsy. It is understandable where this belief in the "personal vibe" comes from. The relationship with certain fund managers can feel like quite a personal one. But, this faith holds many potential pitfalls.

The sector consolidation in the major indexes is so high that periods of weighting stability can easily be misinterpreted as connoting a solid register when really there is little loyalty at all. Appearances can be misleading. If there is a major re-weighting of a sector in the index for reasons unrelated to a company's performance, the company might see its supposed "loyalists" re-weight downwards.

It is not logically in the interests of fund managers to warn management when they are about to become sellers, however loyal they may appear. This only potentially erodes their trading gain. There are also potential vulnerabilities which may force a fund to become a seller but which it does not wish to inform the company about, such as loss of a mandate due to underperformance or a change of fund manager. The competitive nature of the fund management business, imposing shorter mandate lengths, demanding higher performance standards and squeezing fund management costs, means old-fashioned relationship investment is increasingly less realistic. The link between fund and company is likely to become increasingly depersonalised. In this emerging world of institutional investing, the company's shares can possibly become a commodity. In some instances, there may be a real gulf between management perceptions of investor intentions and the reality of what's going on in a fund manager's head.

Towards the notion of investor account management

Given the increasingly exotic mix of institutional investors in the typical register, the complex range of motives and behaviours they exhibit, and the short average period of their investment, what should a manager do to attempt to understand them? I have been highly critical of what our research has shown to be a somewhat complacent "touch and feel" approach to understanding investor motivation. There is often a marked lack of analytical rigour and the absence of sound method. One suggestion that has been proposed by various observers to introduce scientific method is the use of segmentation techniques to group investors into "types". As hopefully we now agree, attempting to "segment" institutional investors in the style of customers does not work in practice. Each fund is unique and will have its own peculiarities, vulnerabilities and goals which may be hard to identify directly. Each fund manager will be under singular pressures and be working to individual goals, which again will be hard to get at.

Rather than attempting to apply segmentation methodologies borrowed from the marketers, managing the relationship with the investor base is best thought of as an "account management" process. The most fundamental step in such an approach is deciding which of the 30–40 institutions on the register really matter? Who is actively driving the price? Each such investor should be researched using objective analytical techniques to identify likely triggers to action, both positive and negative. Gathering much of these data is not straightforward, as fund managers are understandably secretive about their mandates and benchmarks. But, inferences can be drawn from their trading behaviour and investment statements. This is the philosophy I will explore in Chapter 7. It is the foundation stone of a fair value strategy.

The changing nature of institutional fund managers means that old assumptions about behaviour often no longer hold true and the relationship between company and investor is likely to become increasingly more detached and less predictable. A fair value strategy requires a real commitment to resourcing the company to understand and predict investor behaviour. Part of the process of competitive differentiation by any large public company is differentiating the company with investors, which means responding to their "needs" in a targeted manner that reduces the risks of misvaluation. That is where the process of fair value begins.

Part Two

The Building Blocks of Fair Value

4

Towards a fair value strategy

Understanding the fair value process

THE INVESTOR CONTEXT WITHIN WHICH A CEO HAS TO navigate a course for the company is clearly not an easy one. Many institutional fund managers will not be engaged with the company's strategy but be holding the stock because of an index-related strategy. A CEO may invest a huge amount of time trying to influence the behaviour of sections of the investor base, to make them buy into the business strategy, to be party to the value creation process, but much of this effort will be fruitless. It is a little like Lord Leverhulme's quip about his advertising budget – half is wasted but the question is which half? At the same time, they will be under pressure from the intermediary community to promote the growth prospects of the business and to engage in expansionist corporate activity. The implicit (although rarely explicit) goal of corporate strategy will be to maximise the shareprice in as short a time frame as possible. This will probably offer the reward of seeing the company's shareprice appreciate for a while, but it is often creating a rod for every committed stakeholder's back. As we have explored, the cost of misvaluation is high indeed.

Whilst it is only a handful of corporate-level executives who are directly exposed to these investor processes, these same processes have their repercussions deep into the organisation. In the pursuit of shareprice maximisation, decisions are likely to be taken that will tend to favour short-term earnings boosts, such as reduced capital expenditure, constrained spending on training, a bias against start-up "sapling" strategies in favour of stand-alone acquisitions. It is also likely that a deep cross-section of managers will be evaluated and incentivised based on a set of metrics either directly or indirectly linked to shareprice or total shareholder return (TSR). This may be cemented into the fabric through deep commitment to value-based management (VBM) processes. The boom–bust profile of shareprice maximisation strategies is likely, at some point or other, to seriously undermine any VBM programme and may sap the organisation of energy.

Should a company have entered a period of declining shareprice, our research suggests that it will be very hard for the company to recover from a significant discount. We also know that it often requires both a change of strategy and potentially also of management, to persuade shareholders that a re-rating is justified because of renewed potential for growth. For the company these are disruptive changes and many businesses go through them. They consume huge amounts of executive's energy, often resulting in the eye being taken off the business strategy. In such disruptive periods of change, the 5-year strategy cycle is typically abandoned and the company is forced into more short-term reflexes that are perceived to be value-enhancing. At the time of writing, the foremost amongst these is the divestiture of non-core activities in which the company cannot demonstrate immediate advantage. Strategic refocusing is often preceded by management change – something that most management teams should rationally wish to avoid.

Towards the light

So, what is the alternative to suffering stoically at the hands of an imperfect market? Are there ways a large public company can recover and maintain fair value without such dislocating disruption? This is what I call a "fair value strategy". A fair value strategy aims to ensure that the shareprice of the company accurately reflects fundamental long-term value and underlying performance potential. A fair value strategy process begins with understanding where the company currently stands; in other words, is it correctly valued by the markets? See Figure 4.1.

A fundamental tenet of fair value is that management have a clear view of enterprise value, rather than passively assuming that the markets get it right. Does the company have a robust, regularly updated and conservative view of its own enterprise value? Valuation has two component parts – future profitability and the cost of capital needed to finance the generation of profit. On both these measures, management are in principle better positioned than the markets to predict future outcomes. This puts management in a position to take action when premiums and discounts creep into the shareprice.

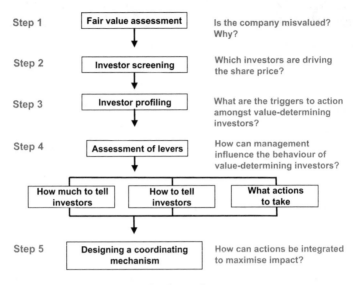

Step 1   Fair value assessment   Is the company misvalued? Why?

Step 2   Investor screening   Which investors are driving the share price?

Step 3   Investor profiling   What are the triggers to action amongst value-determining investors?

Step 4   Assessment of levers   How can management influence the behaviour of value-determining investors?

How much to tell investors   How to tell investors   What actions to take

Step 5   Designing a coordinating mechanism   How can actions be integrated to maximise impact?

Figure 4.1 The fair value process.

A fair value strategy demands that they take active charge of valuation.

This does not mean that management should suddenly be releasing shareprice targets and making forward-looking valuation statements. Almost all sell-side analysts' models are already closely informed by management. This process is conducted discretely and behind the scenes. Allowing the analysts to communicate value targets means, in theory, management can disown them should they wind up missing them and hence create some (although not much) margin for error. It also distances them from any direct legal liability to shareholders for providing forward-looking information. Fair value extends the same processes but demands that management understand more robustly and clearly whether they are being valued correctly. This knowledge has to condition how they manage the relationship with their investors, their brokers and analysts.

So how should management recognise whether their business is fairly valued or not? What in a precise valuation sense does it mean to be fairly valued? The term is bandied around in academic journals but with little specificity beyond some general sense of being "correctly" valued. But what does "correct" mean?

Fair value is defined as existing when market value (I will talk about this specifically in Chapter 5) falls within close range of management's assessment of fundamental value. The first important point is that management need to take responsibility for producing a robust valuation. The second point is the way the degree of acceptable variance between market and fundamental value is established. Is it acceptable for a business to be 10% misvalued, 20%? When does it begin to matter? The test for the range (which will tend to vary sector by sector) is a simple one. Outside this range, misvaluation will typically be sufficient to give rise to external pressures on management to change strategy or direction. If a company can be clearly established to be within this range, it is unlikely to be subject to external pressures for major change. It can then be deemed to be fairly valued. The task of management is to ensure that the company remains within what I call this "fair value corridor".

Our research suggests that the width of the fair value corridor varies substantially sector by sector, ranging from ±25% to ±45%. That is to say, in the first instance cited, management and the market may differ in their estimation of value by 25%

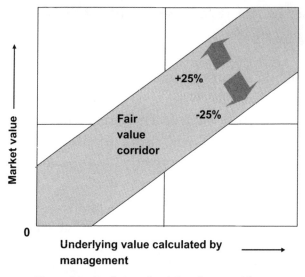

Figure 4.2 Defining the fair value corridor.

either positively or negatively before any external shareholder unrest is felt. Calibrating the corridor correctly is an extremely important, but also demanding task which requires management to apply fair valuation principles which we will consider in detail in Chapter 5.

Having completed the first step of defining the corridor and identifying the company's position in it, the challenge is to make sure the company remains in it or returns to it. The process of staying in the fair value corridor involves three further steps. Step 2 requires management to identify those institutional fund managers who currently set price or who might set price, and who are therefore what I call "value-determining" shareholders. These are the fund managers who drive the index herd and against which management need to focus their attention if they are to remain in the fair value corridor. Identifying them is often far from straightforward and I dedicate a full chapter to this process (Chapter 6).

Step 3 involves building an "account management" function to underpin a thorough understanding of past and likely future fund manager behaviour. The objective of this account management process is two-fold. First, to target management resources where results can be achieved against "value-determining" fund managers. Second, to move away from the anecdotal, personalised approach to understanding and predicting investor behaviour, to an analytical, incremental approach. This should enable management to form clearer views as to why certain fund managers might be behaving as they are, how they might respond to certain events or disclosures and therefore what management might do to alter their perceptions, if at all. Of course, after going through this analysis, many businesses find that they are outside the corridor and are confronted with the challenge of how to return. Here the same broad logic applies.

Of course, none of this analysis is that useful if it is not possible to alter relevant investor perceptions and hence behaviour. In some cases, it may not be possible to alter these outcomes at all, in which case the action steps are clear – engage with the house broker to find a substitute investor better aligned to the value creation strategy of the company. (I will talk about the substitution process in detail presently.) Accordingly, the fourth part of the fair value process is to select the "fair value levers" most likely to prove impactful against these value-determining investors. Some fund managers can be directly influenced by clearer and more compelling explanations of how a strategy will deliver value. Others may even be impacted by a shear increased volume of targeted communications. But, most are likely to be influenced by indirect signals of value. Such signals can take many forms, though from financial signals such as a change in dividend or buy-back policy, through to more complex signals such as the composition of the board or remuneration policy. Fair value levers fall into three broad categories:

- *What we tell investors* – in other words, disclosure of facts and interpretations (e.g., financial performance measures, operating measures, market indexes, strategic objectives, performance guidance, etc.).

- *How we tell investors* – in other words, what communications channels we use, whether direct or indirect (e.g., use of buy-backs and dividends and other signalling devices, selection of different communications mediums, decisions on timing of releases, etc.).

- *What actions we take* – whether we have to resort to fundamental changes to strategy or management to alter perceptions (e.g., changes to non-executive board structure, remuneration policy, capital structure, etc.).

Within each area there is a long list of potential specific levers which we will explore in detail in Part Three. At one point or another in a company's history most value levers will probably have been used. But, based on our research, their impact on fair value is unlikely to have been clearly analysed and they may not have been employed as part of a structured investor strategy. But used in combination and against the right investor triggers, value levers can be powerful tools in delivering a fair value strategy.

Critically, our research would suggest that no single value lever alone tends to be efficacious in maintaining a company in the fair value corridor. There is no silver bullet and indeed the misguided use of certain value levers can be potentially very damaging. Managing a fair value strategy requires a co-ordinated approach among fair value levers which appears absent in many corporate centres. The reason this seems to happen is that different value levers fall under the control of different departments, from strategy through to finance. In many companies, the current investor relations function often does not operate as an adequate coordinating force to draw these strands together. A fair value strategy demands that the company builds a coordinated set of management processes that enable the synchronisation of value levers. Establishing this coordinating mechanism across parent functions can be one of the most challenging aspects of fair value.

The rest of this book takes you step by step through the fair value methodology as an integrated approach to staying in the fair value corridor. However, for some companies, certain modules of the overall methodology will be more immediately relevant than others. Whilst the model is presented as an integrated process, it is legitimate to cherry-pick those pieces that are most pertinent to the company's particular situation rather than follow the entire process through religiously. Indeed, some companies will find they are close to best practice on some areas but lacking in others. The fair value process is not intended to be prescriptive but rather offers a systematic compilation of core methods a company can employ to improve its interaction with shareholders. However, one piece of the fair value approach that cannot be dispensed with, and where our research suggests most companies do not invest sufficient energy, is determining where they are in their fair value corridor. That is where we go next.

5

Determining fair value

How do you know when your company is fairly valued?

HOW SHOULD MANAGEMENT KNOW WHETHER THEIR company is being fairly valued or not? This is truly a thorny challenge and the difficulty of accurately calculating fair value probably explains why few companies appear to invest much resource in managing the internal valuation model and even fewer use their internal model to guide their communications with investors.

There is some irony to this. Our research with a range of senior executives suggested that many are prepared to state with apparent certainty and conviction whether they are undervalued. For obvious reasons, overvaluation was barely mentioned. Yet, when pressed on how they arrived at their conclusion and what fundamental analysis they had at their disposal, there was usually an incomplete response. The few examples we could find of a thorough internal valuation process were episodic, perhaps every few years, and usually done by outside consultants.

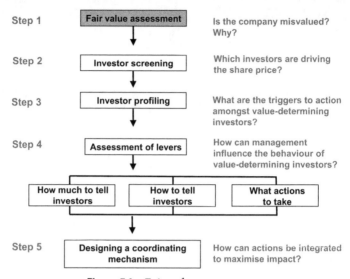

Figure 5.1 Fair value assessment.

Most companies impose a strong influence on the way markets value them. The vast majority of analyst's notes are effectively run via the company for "approval" before they are released, and the company is the primary source for forward-looking information and guidance. Therefore, the company is in effect influencing judgements with not always the most sound basis for doing so. That may partly explain why many analyst's notes prove far too optimistic.

Part of the reason that valuation is not typically an in-house obsession lies in the practical issues surrounding robust valuation. The technical process of valuation is not straightforward. Unless conducted with great rigour, it leaves wide scope for hugely different outcomes and implementing a robust approach requires dedicated expert resource. In the absence of this, some companies rely on sell-side analysts to get their models right which, again, they may not be best positioned to do.

But there may also be another motive that explains why valuation appears often not to be addressed. Accurate valuation poses its own threats. Many companies sitting on large premiums may not own up to it and find ways in their own minds to claim it is not a premium at all or that it is deserved given their prospects. Quite naturally, and in some cases quite rightly, management tend to take an optimistic view of their own prospects. After all, if they don't believe in their own future who will? Of the companies researched as part of this book, 75% claimed to be undervalued as of late 2003, lamenting discounts they felt unable to convince investors really existed. However, when pressed, few could actually produce evidence for this or come up with convincing arguments for how they intended to persuade the markets of the existence of a discount. They might loosely point to a peer competitor on a better rating or turn to historical valuations they had attracted. In general, there was a sense of resignation that management claims of undervaluation, however justifiable, would always be met with cynicism by markets that "often bore no relation to fundamentals". But underlying the frustration was an apparent inability or unwillingness by some management teams to form a robust internal view of value.

This poses a real problem for a management team who, philosophically at least, buys into the concept of fair value. If you don't know what fair value is, how do you know whether you're undervalued or overvalued? How do you know whether the market is over-hyping the stock and increasing the risk of a correction or unjustly penalising it? The cost of misvaluation is potentially very high. Therefore, surely, this issue should be one that keeps all managers up at night? It should be a primary focus of management attention. Yet, oddly, many companies seem to lack the factual basis on which to make this judgement.

It is clear that management cannot simply lean back and let the analysts do the valuation work. We have already discussed the problem of relying on the market as a perfect arbitrator of value – that the market is not perfect and for entirely rational reasons. In this unreliable valuation environment, two things are clear. First, that management need to play an active lead role in ensuring they are fairly valued. They can no longer obfuscate and blame the analysts for getting it wrong. Second, to do so, they need a more robust approach to gauging whether they are creating value and whether the markets are accurately interpreting their efforts.

Enter the valuation game

Institutional fund managers and their advisors use a number of standard tools to gauge value. Broadly speaking, these measures divide into two camps – absolute measures of value and relative measures of value. Let's start with absolute measures. Absolute measures of value attempt to estimate value according to an intrinsic logic of what the company is worth, whether based on EBITDA, CFROI, EVA, DCFs, or any other number of exotic flavours of measurement. One way or another, most of these absolute measures relate back to a company's cashflow. How much cashflow is the company likely to produce into the future and what risk or cost is attached to this cashflow?

The reason for picking cashflow rather than accrual-based earnings is two-fold. To isolate fundamental value, investors are concerned to identify what, should the company distribute its free cashflow to shareholders from now into perpetuity, would be their cashflow return on investment. Whilst in practice this never happens as management place demands on at least a substantial part of the cashflow, it does give a clear indication of the value that might be available to owners of the business. The second reason cashflow is favoured is that, whilst earnings as an accounting measure can be manipulated, cashflow cannot so readily be engineered.

Accrual-based earnings are premised on assumptions about revenue recognition and timing, assumptions about treatment of costs as either expenses or capital items, assumptions about depreciation and amortisation of assets, assumptions about treatment of exceptional items and, most topically, assumptions about pension fund returns. The potential sources of "discretion", even if done out of honourable intentions of "smoothing", are large indeed. Most companies are entirely scrupulous in their intent but, under pressure to meet quarterly targets, all engage in some level of "earnings management". Cashflow, by contrast, is a fairly tightly defined measure and can be directly reconciled to earnings. However, even cashflow is subject to reporting discretion.

Cashflow measurements come in many flavours. American investors, and particularly private equity investors, favour

EBITDA as a proxy for cashflow which excludes treatment of capital items including working capital. Others favour free cashflow after capital expenditure (CAPEX). Whichever particular method is used, thorny assumptions have to be made about sustainable levels of capital investment and R&D. Assumptions also have to be made about treatment of acquisitions. Should cashflow from acquired companies be included or is organic cashflow the only real indicator of growth? There is also the issue of the interpretation of the working capital cycle. Is the dynamic of working capital likely to remain as it is? Will net working capital deteriorate as markets get more competitive? What about set-asides for future pension fund shortfalls? Has appropriate account been made of bad debts and credit risk? As any good analyst asks questions about what is included and what excluded, cashflow can look far more slippery than it first appears.

Of course, earnings and cashflow both hold the same fundamental dilemma when it comes to the use of historical measures to project future outcomes. All valuations are typically premised on a minimum 5-year projection, extrapolated from historical numbers but incorporating insight into future competitive dynamics. Will competitive dynamics alter, taking margins and revenue growth with them? Will strains on working capital and capital expenditure change dramatically from the historical pattern? Will R&D investments really translate into revenue? It is the weakness of all forward-looking valuations that they rely on projections from historical patterns when the evidence suggests that the past is no certain guide to the future. The impact that variances in different assumptions about the future create on valuation are potentially huge.

The projection of cashflows or some proxy for cashflows is only part of the valuation story. In addition, there is the issue of the cost of capital to fund these cashflows. The primary method used to assess the cost of capital to fund future cashflows is the calculation of the weighted average cost of capital or WACC. The cost of capital of any business is a combination of the cost of equity and the cost of debt, which will be weighted differently in different businesses. The cost of debt is an easy calculation, as corporate will be charged with, and in turn charge on at divisional level, a quantifiable rate for the debt. The hard part is the cost of equity or what investors expect as a return on their cash, reflecting the risk of their investment. Accepted wisdom says that the best way of calculating the equity element of the WACC is using the Capital Asset Pricing Model or CAPM.[1] But again, despite the great energies poured into refining this tool by analysts and academics, it remains fundamentally spongy and uncrisp.

The WACC calculated using the CAPM methodology has three critical components – the risk-free rate, the risk premium associated with stocks in general and the beta. The risk-free rate equates to the rate on a government-backed, triple-A-rated security such as a Gilt or Treasury Note. The risk premium measures the market return expected by investors holding equities in general or of a particular class (e.g., large-cap stocks that comprise the FTSE 100 and 250) over and above the risk-free rate as compensation for the incremental risk. Both the premium and risk-free rate can be measured at any point in time and effectively in real time by looking at the prevailing rates. As

[1] See Brealey and Myers (1996) for a full review of CAPM.

they reflect the sentiment of the market as a whole, the level of possible error is far less than it would be for an individual stock, although such market-wide errors do occur. Comparisons with historical market averages can dampen such errors to a significant extent. The risk-free rate will move in line with interest rates and the risk premium has tended historically to remain within fairly tight bounds. There is at least some basis to believe that the immediate future of both is moderately predictable and both measures can be struck as currently as possible. Besides, there is nothing the individual analyst or manager can do to alter or manipulate them. Everyone is bound by the same statistics.

The beta, by contrast, is mainly company-specific, measuring the historical movement of the company's shares against its sector or the market as a whole. The problem with this aspect of the CAPM is that use of the beta makes a huge leap of faith that the company's relative volatility will in the future follow the same pattern as it has in the past. There is far less certainty over this assumption than with the risk-free rate and equity risk premium. Also, there is far more discretion in terms of how it is measured. Is it volatility of the shares v. its competitor set, its sector, the market as a whole? Which is more appropriate in each case? And over what time period should it be averaged? One week, one month, one year? The field for error is wide open.

Cashflow valuation is hugely sensitive to a change in the discount rate and the discount rate in turn is highly influenced by the beta chosen. A 1% variance in the discount rate will create around a 10% valuation difference and a 1% variance in the beta will produce a similar variance in the discount rate. Most companies put significant effort into calculating the appropriate discount rate or cost of capital and this measure can typically be narrowed down to a reasonably tight range, no wider than, say, 3% variance. However, even this level of error can radically effect a valuation and it is a weakness all valuation processes have to accommodate.

As a consequence of all this uncertainty, gauging absolute value is no trivial undertaking. It requires expertise and time. Most of this expertise resides with the investment banks and brokers. The analyst community run "models" of discounted cashflow which form the bread and butter of their trade. And on this basis they calculate what they believe the shares of companies should be worth. Typically, most Investor Relations (IR) directors also designate an individual in the team to review lead analyst's models in an attempt to ensure that no obvious miscalculations are being made. It is fairly unusual for an analyst to put out a forecast on value without the company's tacit, although unstated approval. Not surprisingly therefore, most lead analyst's public valuations of a particular company tend to fall within a close range.

If, by contrast, you took three models of a single company run entirely without knowledge of the other by three different analysts, they may produce valuations with a dispersal of 30–40%. That is to say, whilst one model may put a company's worth at 100, another will be at 70 and so on. The source of the variance does not usually lie in the technique. A proportion may lie in the discount rate but there tends to be a fairly uniform rate applied by each analyst to each company and in some cases the company will make public its own calculations of the WACC.

The bulk of the discrepancy typically lies in the underlying assumptions about cashflow and, in particular, growth in cashflow. A 5% difference in estimates of future growth in cashflow produce a 40% impact on value. A 10% variance in estimates of future growth will potentially produce close to a 100% difference in value. The longer cashflows are projected out, and the less clear the assumptions made about the competitive context, then the greater is the room for variance.

The basis of valuation tends to be the same across most analysts – a 5-year annual projection of cashflow and then a perpetuity calculation in the fifth year. The primary variance in forecasts tends to lie in assumptions surrounding the perpetuity or terminal value. In most cashflow models, cashflows are projected out for 5 years based on bottom-up estimates by division, reflecting some sort of robust business logic and market analysis. But, thereafter, it is a finger in the air. Only a few businesses are able to hazard a reliable guess at performance more than 5 years out. Even presumably stable entities such as Shell have proved unreliable at estimating such a fixed and quantifiable asset as their reserves of oil and hence future production. Since more than half of a total valuation usually resides in the perpetuity, assumptions about the terminal year are critical. This is where the subjectivity really sets in with many valuation processes.

Most managers are wary of over-forecasting for next year, but for the next decade is another matter. It is too distant and abstract to feel accountable about. Human nature tends to be far less conservative when it comes to punting on very distant events. The more distant the time horizon the more we are prepared to take a view. In general, our research would suggest that sell-side analysts will tend to assume higher growth rates into perpetuity than they will a year out. As recently as March 2003 the average FTSE forecast assumed an implicit growth rate into perpetuity of almost 20% in an environment of less than 3% GDP growth. Management can be complicit in over-aggressive growth forecasts, particularly when it comes to time frames for which they are unlikely to be held accountable. After all, the role of managing has to be an optimistic one. Who would happily forecast declining margins and market share over 10 years? Surely, opportunities will arise to lift anaemic growth? This sort of optimism may account for the widespread sensation of being undervalued amongst those managers we interviewed. But it also wreaks havoc with the concept of fair value. When it comes to the perpetuity calculation in particular, intense conservativeness is critical if it is not to be self-deluding.

It's all relative

It is perhaps understandable that, given all these uncertainties and traps, most companies and analysts do not actually rely on fundamental assessments of value at all. Instead, their attention is focused on relative value and above all their price earnings ratio or "rating". Most senior management are acutely attuned to their PE and treat it as their principle barometer of the competitive position of their business. The virtue of the PE is that it is very easy to calculate and very easy to compare across a sector and any index. Analysts may talk endlessly about sophisticated cashflow models but, when push comes to shove, they all rely on earnings multiples to determine what a company is worth. This is surprisingly true of investment bankers and deal makers also who are often attributed with more fundamental assessments of value. But they all return to PEs.

This fact alone is enough to ensure that management are primarily attuned to their valuation relative to their peer group and sector rather than their absolute value. The fact that most institutional fund managers focus on relative weightings of stocks v. the index and v. the sector simply reinforces this. There are many off-shoots of the PE such as EBITDA multiples, EBIT multiples, and EBITA multiples, but they are all founded on the same principle – that relative not absolute value is what matters. Who is to say what something is fundamentally worth? All that matters is what someone else is willing to pay for it.

The focus on relative measures of value gives rise to a number of thorny issues. The first question thrown up by the use of relative valuation is relative to what? Most fund managers measure value relative to peer groups – companies competing in the same sector of a similar size. The markets themselves are essentially structured around sectoral peer groups and this is how shareprice data are often organised, particularly in the press, such as the FT. It is no coincidence that most funds are managed by reference to sector weightings. Sectoral indexes make life easier for the fund manager. First, they decide how they will weight the sector v. the index and then how they will weight each company v. its sector. But such relative measures can actually make life harder for the company.

Often it is not at all clear to management against what bench-marks they are being measured by key institutional fund managers or whether these are the right benchmarks. As index management has become all-pervasive, so the number of indexes has proliferated as funds have sought to differen-tiate themselves – from European indexes, through to hi-tech, blue-chip, growth, value, corporate and social responsibility and commodity indexes, to name but a few. If ten fund managers in the stock are following three different index strategies with three different sets of benchmark peers, then it can be a major challenge for management making any sense of their motives or attempting to influence perceptions of the company.

Typically, companies make little proactive attempt to set the peer group against which they believe they should be measured. They sort of assume everyone knows who they are and who their competitors are, which is often a mistake. Depending on the relevant peer group, their relative valuation will be interpreted very differently. For example, marketing services companies are rated differently from support services companies, often by as much as 30%, although many of the companies are actually quite interchangeable in what they deliver to their customer or client. Often, it is not clear at all whether a particular company should really sit in one index or peer grouping v. another. An IT company supplying handset software could be construed to be a telecom company. An oil company focused on drilling and prospecting could be construed to be a mining company rather than a business founded on consumer-led distribution and retail. A travel promotions business could be engaged in a media communications-related activity or supply passenger services. The capital markets tend to slot firms into groupings, but sometimes these groupings are not necessarily the natural home of a particular company.

This issue of peer group selection becomes even more complicated when natural global peers are quoted on different exchanges and have no real counterpart on their own exchange. Can WPP really be compared against large media stocks in the UK, such as Pearson, when its real advertising rivals Omnicom and Interpublic are listed in New York? Who is Vodafone's real peer? This means that the decision about what is the appropriate peer group is vital, and sometimes better understood by the company than by the broadly focused fund manager whose fund may be nationally orientated.

Another challenge with relative valuation and PE multiples is that there is no surety that 15 times earnings or 20 times earnings is a correct valuation. In a theoretical world, there would be a direct relationship between the growth prospects of their earnings and the multiples that companies are awarded. In order to warrant a multiple of 30, a business would need to show high, double-digit growth into the foreseeable future. As a rough rule of thumb, the multiple attached to a company should correlate broadly to its anticipated rate of growth in earnings per share. But, in practice PEs do not obey the scientific rules of the theoretical world.

In the world of relative valuation, stock values are set by relative not absolute performance. In a high-performing peer group, 20% growth may meet with a shareprice fall. If a company's shares perform notably worse than the sector index, irrespective of the company's underlying performance, then thcy will be punished automatically. 'I'he rules of relative performance quickly frustrate people who are focused on absolute performance, such as the typical line manager. In a world of imperfect markets they introduce a variable that can appear unmanageable and also obsessive. All one can say on the basis of a PE is that a company's value bears this or that relationship to the general market and to other comparable stocks. In times of general equity, inflation 20 times earnings may be a bad rating. In bear markets it may be a resounding endorsement that management are doing something right.

Lastly, there is of course the issue of the earnings measure which forms the denominator of the PE calculation. Different companies will clearly have different interpretations of generally accepted accounting principles, and will take different attitudes to revenue recognition, treatment of certain costs, the aggressiveness of depreciation schedules, including goodwill, and the adequacy of pension provisions, to name but a few. The earnings number used in the PE calculation will also tend to be a forward full-year number and hence subject to the vagaries of annual forecasts. The result can be reasonable questionableness as to whether PEs are truly comparable and give a reliable guide to relative value.

So, what are management to read into multiples? They clearly say something about the market. But, they can say far less of value about the company. They do not tell management what they are really worth in any absolute sense. It is clearly vital that the company understands what peer group its primary institutional investors are measuring it against. It is also vital that it closely monitors its movements against its peer group. A diminution of PE relative to its peers is likely to be a key trigger for action by some of its core holders. As such, it is a warning mechanism and guiding device towards general sentiment. Indeed, more systematic analysis of relative valuation can give important insights into why a company is being misvalued. For example, it may be due to overall sector ratings being depressed or peer group companies souring the sector with underperformance.

As such, every company needs to be thorough in regularly reviewing its relative position. This will involve selecting the relevant peer group against which its primary investors measure it, itself often requiring some thorough research. It then needs to track its shareprice, its relative PE, the relative volume of its shares traded (Table 5.1). It is also wise to monitor basic relative performance metrics as illustrated in Figure 5.2 and Table 5.2, as well as perform basic analysis to understand the relationship between the company's PE and its relative performance (Figure 5.3). This may offer relatively easy insight into basic influences on shareholder perceptions as well as insight into competition for the investor pound.

Towards the fair value corridor

We have talked about the dangers that arise when fundamental value and market value diverge. Relying on relative valuation, as easy as it may be, is not adequate. It is critical that management understand whether the company's

Table 5.1 Basic market comparators

Peer group	Shareprice (£)	Market CAP (£m)	Shares traded (%)	Latest EPS(p)	Dividend yield (%)	P/E	Major announcements?	Analyst re-rating?
Company A	1.26	1,126	2.6	2.62	3.1	17	None	None
Company B	1.96	221	2.1	3.31	2.6	24	None	Upgrade from Merrill Lynch
Company C	1.03	873	1.6	2.21	1.7	14	None	None
Company D	1.97	3,151	1.8	3.26	3.6	28	None	None
Sector index or average	N/A	N/A	1.9	2.96	2.7	22	None	None

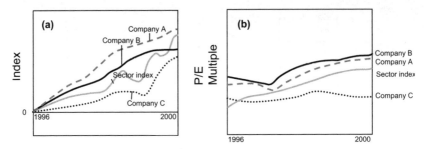

Figure 5.2   Basic market comparators. (a) Shareprice performance v. peers & sector index. (b) Relative valuation v. peers & sector index.

Table 5.2   Average weekly percentage of shares traded

Week	1	2	3	4	5	6	7	8	9	10
Company A	2.1	4	2.1	1.9	2	1.6	3	2	5	2.6
Company B	2.6	2.7	2.9	3.1	4	3.2	0.4	4	5	8
Company C	1	0.5	0.2	0	0.7	1	1.2	1	2	1
Sector index	2.2	2.8	1.9	2.1	2.9	2.3	1.2	3	2	3

As percentage of shares in issue.

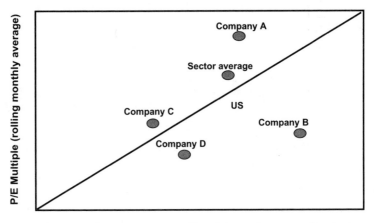

Figure 5.3   Basic market comparators. Possible performance dimensions.
  1   EPS (forecast full year)
  2   EPS growth (2 yr/5 yr)
  3   Dividend yield (forecast full year)
  4   Gearing (Debt ÷ Equity × 100)
  5   Operating margin (%).

absolute market value is an accurate reflection of its under-lying cash creation potential. To do so, management have to closely monitor the relationship between market value and their own internal, conservative estimates of underlying or fair value. The primary dashboard indicator of fair value is a very simple matrix of the market value against management's estimate of value.

As we discussed in Chapter 4, the relationship between market value and management's assessment of fundamental value is rarely a linear one. Indeed, there may not be a close fit at all. This relationship has a level of flexibility in it which I call the fair value corridor. But, there comes a point where the divergence is great enough that it will demand manage-ment action, either because of the risk of correction from a position of overvaluation or because undervaluation will cause the board and eventually fund managers to push for change. Most management teams will have a feel for these outer limits of the corridor. In some sectors, typically where share volatility is high, the corridor may be quite wide. In others it will be tight. Management's task is to manage the company into the corridor and ensure it stays there.

Our research suggests that in most cases this corridor is typically about 50° wide; that is to say that a discrepancy of greater than 25% either up or down produces tension between management and active fund managers and tends to demand action be taken by management to narrow the value gap. Our observation from a number of sectors is that, in today's volatile market for shares, this barrier is often breached, although companies sometimes don't know it. It is unclear whether on average the corridor is widening as a result of such volatility or narrowing.

In principle, management should be in a good position (and better positioned than any outsider) to estimate the value of their business based on a well-informed, conservative and clear-minded view of the long-term potential of the company. Of course, whilst the inside view promises insight, it can also come loaded with bias. Accurate valuation relies on the calculation of an accurate cost of capital and sustainable assumptions about margins and growth. The problem is these constraints are not always imposed by management teams. The budgeting process of companies can easily inflate growth and underestimate risk, particularly when it comes to the calculation of acquired revenue streams. Enthusiasm, combined with self-interest, can win out over sobriety.

As things stand, management rarely take responsibility for measuring and overtly providing clear guidance on value to analysts based on thorough analysis. Few companies invest much resource in maintaining a robust internal valuation model based on conservative assumptions. More typically, they will episodically hire consultants to paint a snapshot at a point in time which quickly gets abandoned as events overtake it. Therefore, they rely on the analyst process as a crutch.

In the case of companies who do maintain an internal valuation model, fundamental valuations tend to emerge from the strategy process, and not from the budgeting and reforecasting round. The annual budgeting round is the foundation stone for annual performance targeting which drives compensation, capital expenditure and also communications with the financial markets, hence setting market expectations. The budgeting round is something in which companies invest huge energies. It tends to be highly internally consultative – involving a series of review cycles with divisional heads. It is a fluid and iterative process that can adapt to change through the financial year and also to changes in external expectations. Its hallmark is the all-too-familiar battle cry of Q3, "We've got to squeeze out more profit; I don't care how you do it ..."

By contrast, the 3–5-year planning cycle which gives birth to the valuation process is usually owned by the strategy department. It is built up on the basis of fairly cerebral interactions with the "thinkers" around the company. Not that it isn't taken seriously, but it doesn't tend to have the pragmatic teeth of the budgeting cycle – it is more remote, internally focused and often meant to stimulate growth initiatives rather than hold managers to delivery targets. It can form part of the investor communications process but is usually ancillary to the budgeting and reforecasting cycle, if for no other reason than lack of bandwidth on company and investor's parts.

Understandably, as a result, the strategy cycle tends to receive lower priority from the CEO and CFO than the budgeting process. The director of strategy charged with this process is often not on the board. The finance director who ultimately owns the budget cycle is. The CFO has investor contact, the strategy director does not. Nor does the strategy process tend to be as externally consultative and as responsive to investor feedback. It is the CFO who ultimately controls the investor relations process. For these reasons, the strategy valuation model will tend to carry less credibility as an arbiter of value, both internally and externally.

Also, it is not always the case that the strategy process results in a valuation model at all. Often its objectives are articulated in terms of marketplace measures and strategic goals, but not enterprise value and shareprice. And even if a model does emerge, often on the back of consultancy projects supported by an external strategy advisor, such as McKinsey or BCG, it can suffer the weakness of being rigid and quickly redundant in fast-moving commercial settings. To keep it updated means dedicating resource or continuing to employ consultants, something companies are often reluctant to do.

It is this void that the house broker fills. What model there is often resides with the house broker. The community with the most active valuation models tend to be the sell-side analysts. They hone them, test them and update them regularly. The caveat with this, as we have already discussed, is that such models tend to be optimistic and can overstate future growth. They have not empirically always proved a reliable guide to fair value. They are often marketing tools and not in-house analytical tools to support investor strategy. Most companies are judicious in their management of analysts even if it is known they are overoptimistic. There is the fear that a bad word will prompt a poor rating and a stock fall. The analysts have the psychological upper hand – they are better paid, more mobile and managing sector coverage rather than just one company. Leaving it to the analysts is the far easier option for most executives.

There is also an appropriate wariness on the part of the company regarding the regulatory context of determining and communicating value. A director of IR is typically cautious about being publicly seen to get involved in directly guiding valuations. Management assiduously avoid being pinned down to future earnings numbers, just in case fund managers turn on them for failure to deliver. It is entirely understandable given the high-profile demise of many large enterprises at the hands of investor suits, notably in the USA. Instead, the chosen route is the analyst briefing. If this is the only viable route for management to take, which in most cases it probably is, the question is how closely do they steer and guide based on a robust internal model?

In the absence of close management, some analysts will tend to over-rate. If they are bullish on the company, conservative principles surrounding the valuation process may fall away. Conversely, a company with low or negative analyst following will tend to suffer disproportionately and again lose contact with fair value principles on the downside. Management need to actively guide based on carefully honed information and analysis and not leave it to chance, even if this means disappointing the lead analyst, painful as that may appear at the time.

Towards fair valuation rules

Hopefully, I have gone some way to convincing you that it is essential that management take responsibility for managing their own valuation model and use it to guide external expectations through the medium of the analyst. This may not sound the greatest breakthrough, but it is a critical change in mindset from an ostensibly passive position (an investor call is a bad call), to an active one – investors are there to be "managed". Valuation has to be transformed into a core process and made relevant, flexible and above all robust. It has to be complemented by relative valuation measures but must not be replaced by them.

The starting point of the fair value process is to change the way the valuation process is tied into other management processes. The core financial process is the budgeting cycle which has the virtue of being driven from divisional budgets and being subject to a robust reforecasting process. The budgeting process is typically limited to 1 year out, broken down monthly and reviewed quarterly. By contrast, the 5-year planning cycle is completely divorced in many companies from the annual budgeting cycle. It is fairly static and non-consultative. It is quickly rendered inaccurate and obsolete, other than for giving general direction. Hence, it cannot be the unique home of valuation.

The fair value process begins by tying the valuation process back into the budgeting cycle. Fair value requires projection of performance out at least 5 years to produce any accuracy of measurement. These forecasts are best derived as part of the budgeting cycle, as an adjunct in the form of a 5-year rolling "plan". Like the budget, this plan is best constructed at divisional level based on the same aggregation process as the budgeting cycle. In other words, its foundation is to be found amongst those people who actually have a feel for the businesses. It should ideally be subject to the same reforecasting process as the budget, but at a minimum would be revised bi-annually with the commencement and half-year reforecast of the budgeting cycle. It should also be subject to a similar level of enquiry and consultation.

This automatically requires that the 5-year rolling plan is taken as seriously as the budget and managers perceive themselves to be held to it with the same accountability they are held to their budgets. In this way, the 5-year plan should become "owned" by divisional management, rather than residing in the ether of strategy at corporate. Such a process of pushing down responsibility for the plan has a large number of implications for training and also compensation, which I will come to presently.

The primary benefit of pushing down forecasting is that divisional management have more chance of defusing overshoots. If line management are held accountable for the 5-year plan, in the same way they are for the budget, they are likely to be more conservative. The dynamic of conservativeness is usually observable in well-run companies when it comes to the annual budget. Good managers will tend to hold back projected earnings so that they are sure to hit or exceed the targets corporate gives them. In the context of 5-year projections this type of conservativeness is an essential counter-balance to the habit of assuming aggressive growth into the future for which management know they cannot be held accountable in the immediate term. The objective should be "sane", and achievable projections of cashflow for the following 5-year period updated every 6 months as competitive and other pressures impact the budget.

Once the valuation and budgeting cycles are reunited, there are a number of important conditions that apply to it if it is to conform to fair value principles. First, the core denominator of measurement is cashflow. Often, line managers are not familiar with converting earnings-based forecasts into cashflow-based forecasts. Many will not be familiar with reviewing the balance sheet or have focused energies on issues, such as net working capital and capital employed. Indeed, a balance sheet may not even be habitually compiled at divisional level. Most budgeting, reporting and control systems are entirely P&L-oriented.

The discipline of integrating a cashflow line into the budgeting cycle is beneficial in its own right. It focuses attention on capital expenditure which is often treated as a separate branch of negotiations from the core budget. It also focuses attention on the issue of net working capital and, particularly, the speed with which receivables are collected and also the thorny issue of bad debt. Above all, it reduces wriggle room for playing the accounting games of revenue and cost recognition. Because cashflow timings and accrued earnings behave differently, with cashflow typically lagging earnings, cashflow measurement is likely to force a longer than 12-month view of the world, as a healthy balance to the annual P&L straitjacket. The addition of a cashflow forecast line to existing P&L lines is not complicated and does not raise any huge IT burden. But, what it does demand is a developed approach to estimating uncertain future events.

Down to some nitty-gritty

The exact specification of the financial model a company may develop for valuation purposes is not something I will go into in detail. A large number of tailored approaches exist, sold by consulting firms ranging from McKinsey to BCG to Marsh McClellan. All are based on discounted cashflow analysis and each has its own twists and turns. In developing an outstanding internal valuation model, there are consequently a large number of places the company can turn to for advice on building its model. Whatever the chosen model, what does matter are the principles laid down by the company about how core inputs into the model are measured. This is where fair value has much to say.

The starting point of the valuation process is the 5-year cashflow projection or plan. This should be done at SBU level and then aggregated by division in precisely the same way as the budget. Most business managers are able to form a reasonably sane view of the business 5 years out and, if held accountable, will employ reasonable rules of prudence. They are likely to assume maintenance or slight improvement in operating margins, reasonable revenue growth, status quo in terms of trade or net working capital. They may be leery about deducting sufficient capital expenditures, despite the fact that depreciation will have been added back as a non-cash item. They will probably not integrate acquired revenues and earnings at the SBU or divisional level, and this should also be avoided at the corporate level also. Once these 5-year forecasts are aggregated at corporate level and appropriate corporate overhead cost is applied, the 5-year plan should be subject to the same iterative review as the budget, so that a definitive and conservative plan is arrived at.

The real challenge of valuation lies in the treatment of the terminal year or perpetuity. Perpetuity calculation is where much of the enterprise value will lie, even up to as much as 70% of it. This is where the company pursuing a fair value strategy needs to lay down clear guidelines for purposes of its own modelling as well as for divisional managers contributing to the plan in five key areas:

- Revenue growth.

- Operating margins.

- Net working capital.

- Capital expenditure.

- Calculation of the WACC.

Perhaps the most critical of these is revenue growth, where a 1% difference in assumptions can produce a 7–10% difference in terminal values. The governing fair value rule is that perpetuity organic growth will not exceed the long-term average GDP growth of the primary national markets of the company, unless divisional management can put forward a compelling argument that this will not be the case. In general, only one-fifth of large corporates consistently beat GDP growth over a 20-year period in their primary markets, even though analyst forecasts often assume far higher organic rates of growth. Of course, much of the top-line growth of large companies comes from acquisitions which are often implicitly factored into perpetuity calculations – *"If things slow down, we'll do a few deals. There are so many of them anyway, we're turning the bankers away in droves ..."*. However, the statistics point clearly to the unreliability of acquisitions as substitutes for a

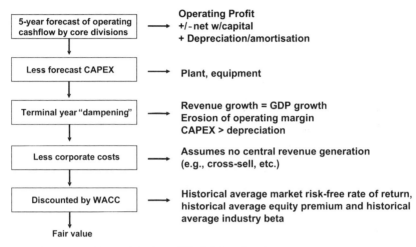

Figure 5.4 Simplified fair valuation process.

robust and growing core business, however tempting a solution it might be to redeem anaemic growth. For this reason, non-organic revenue growth is excluded from the perpetuity calculation as part of fair value principles.

Operating margins have, similarly, to be treated with great conservativeness. It is likely that, over time, operating margins in the core will decline as competitive pressures reduce pricing, and new products erode the profitability of exiting "cash cows". Fair value principles require the imposition of a "decay function" to average operating margins across a business which will tend to erode perpetuity margins to at or below the average margin for a mature business in the particular sector. Where this margin will wind up is case-specific, and determining what is a mature margin will require detailed competitor analysis. Once again, divisional management may provide a compelling argument why this is not the case and erosion can be countered through specific innovation. This argument must be tested rigorously as it will fundamentally alter enterprise value.

Converting these operating margins into cashflow requires assumptions to be made about long-term movements in working capital. Most long-term management assumptions assume a net neutral working capital position into perpetuity. In other words, they assume that there will be no deterioration of net receivables or work in progress, no deterioration in credit quality and no tightening up by suppliers. This assumption is highly optimistic as it assumes no change in supplier or buyer power. Fair value principles require that there be an assumption of deterioration in trading terms as the industry matures, and the supply chain consolidates. Buyers will slow down payment and suppliers will apply pressure to future payments as they consolidate and automate. As a result, there will be a net charge to cashflow to fund working capital. This charge might range anywhere from between 1% and 10% of net working capital, again depending on the strength of the argument that can be put forward by divisional management about their ability to counter any such deterioration. The decision about the size of the net deterioration will be highly impactful on cashflow and valuation.

Finally, perpetuity calculations often fail to reflect the impact of capital expenditure, assuming that this will be offset by the add-back of depreciation in the cashflow calculation. The assumption that CAPEX and depreciation offset each other usually emanates from a mindset that says maturing businesses demand less capital expenditure and will tend to transform themselves into cash cows. In other words, they will produce capital rather than consume it. This is a very dangerous assumption for purposes of a perpetuity as it can dramatically inflate cashflow expectations. In order to sustain a large business into perpetuity against mounting competitive pressures, it is likely that a business will have to invest ahead of depreciation, with core assets requiring renewal faster than the average depreciation schedule of 20 years.

Fair value principles suggest that CAPEX exceed depreciation by between 5% and 20%, again depending on the argument divisional management can mount to counter this assumption. Divisional management will be accustomed to negotiating with the corporate centre over CAPEX as an adjunct to the budgeting round. But, they will not typically be accustomed to thinking about the relationship between CAPEX and depreciation rates and how this relates to future cashflows. Linking the capital budgeting process to the valuation plan may help avoid this problem to some extent.

The net effect of fair value principles on expectations for growth, profitability, working capital and capital expenditure will be to dampen the perpetuity calculation in line with conservative principles. Since more than half of normal valuations reside in the terminal value, the treatment of the terminal year is critical to fair value, and it is here that the robustness of the internal valuation model will be made or lost. Whatever precise model a particular company adopts to measure cashflow at the operating level, the principles of fair value will be an essential underpinning of an accurate valuation.

The consolidation of cashflow from a divisional level typically exposes the thorny issue of the contribution of the corporate centre to group costs and performance. Typically, corporate-level costs and associated cashflow are not broken out separately from total group performance. Perhaps understandably, there is often a level of nervousness on the part of group-level management with exposing the corporate centre to cost/benefit analysis by shareholders.

The challenge facing corporate-level managers in all companies is can they create more value from the whole than the individual business could if they were independent? If they can't, the corporate parent has no role. Historically, most corporates were very leery indeed about talking about how much value they directly contribute in addition to the independent value generating activities of the companies they own. Very few engaged in break-up analysis and few investors were given sufficiently desegregated information to make the calculation with real accuracy for themselves.

Corporate costs typically amount to between 2% and 5% of group revenues and hence have a material impact on margins and cashflow, particularly in a mature business with single-digit operating margins. It is not atypical for analysts to assume that the incremental benefits of "synergies" and cross-sell will offset any corporate cost which can therefore be excluded, particularly from the perpetuity calculation. Fair value principles would hold that the full cost of corporate be expensed against cashflow, with no offsetting assumption about incremental revenue unless corporate management can make a very strong argument otherwise. The logic mirrors that of divisional and SBU management. Be conservative about the future unless there is a compelling argument to the contrary. Since few corporate centres create revenue, it is only usually safe to assume it is a cost centre.

Back to WACC . . .

This leaves one thorny issue for the valuation process – the weighted average cost of capital. A decade ago most management teams would have been very unfamiliar with the notion of the cost of capital. Today, prompted by the rise of value-based management, the notion that capital has a cost which should be deducted from cashflow is commonplace. The goal of quoted companies is to beat their own cost of capital. Some companies now even provide a statement of the cost of capital in their annual report.

The most conservative analyst might argue that, as far as perpetuity is concerned, it would be wise to assume that the return on equity the business will achieve is unlikely to exceed its cost of capital. This would essentially knock out the value attributed to perpetuity. This cannot be a correct assumption in most circumstances. Most businesses have a value creation life beyond 5 years, meaning they can exceed their cost of capital and make a positive return to share-holders. This should logically result in an increase in share-price over time which is what we observe in the case of most large businesses that have been quoted for a while. For purposes of fair value, it would be hoped that, having applied the fair valuation principles outlined above, the business is able to beat its cost of capital and therefore increase its value into perpetuity. Determining whether this is so or not relies on an accurate calculation of the cost of capital.

As with other aspects of cashflow valuations, the methods for calculating the cost of capital are well explored and have been refined by many commentators and financiers. The issue is deciding what variant of these models to adopt, usually with the advice of the broker or consultant, and then applying conservative principles that do not inflate value by understating risk.

As we have discussed, the average cost of equity of a business is typically calculated using the Capital Asset Pricing Model or CAPM, and the CAPM has three core components to it – the risk premium implicit in shares, the risk-free rate and the beta. The beta is where most of the measurement discretion lies in calculating the cost of capital. The beta is typically measured by calculating the volatility of the company's shareprice v. the market as a whole or a particular sector. If it is more volatile, so the discount rate will rise to reflect greater systematic risk. We have noted that it is also an inherently backward-looking measure, based on past performance v. the market or sector. The CAPM calculation, and hence the discount rate, is very sensitive to assumptions regarding the beta.

The challenge occurs when you consider whether a company's historical volatility is a reliable guide to its future volatility. The markets in general suffer many pricing imperfections, and individual stocks can suffer large and regular pricing aberrations. The movements in an individual stock v. the index may not reflect accurately, or indeed at all, long-term prospects for the company. Therefore, historical betas may be a poor guide to the risk connected with future cashflows. The risk of a beta giving a distorted insight into future risk will increase if the beta is measured, as it often is, over short historical periods, such as 1 year or less.

Fair value principles posit that a key assumption be made that the systematic risk associated with the company will revert to its longer term historical average, and that this average should in reasonable circumstances closely mirror that of its analogous peer group. In practical terms, this means that the beta used should be averaged over the past 5 years, and that, should there be divergence with the analogous peer group, then this in turn should be averaged with the average of this group. The result is an assumption: that in the absence of clearer insight (perhaps from the broker), the risk connected with the company's future cashflows will tend towards the historical average of the sector in which it operates.

Looking into the crystal ball

The compounding effect of fair value principles on valuation is typically to dampen over-exuberant forecasts of future profitability (Figure 5.5). This dampening effect may be quite strong in some circumstances and involve a large downward revision of enterprise value. But, it will also mean that expectations, both internally and externally, are more soberly calibrated and future value shocks are hopefully diffused upfront. The result should be that expectations can be

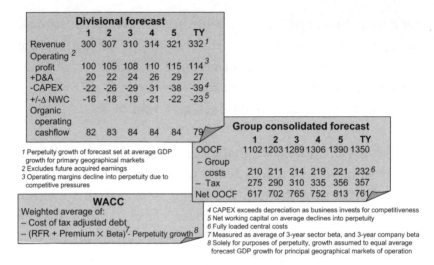

Figure 5.5 Illustrative fair valuation summary.

WACC = Weighted Average Cost of Capital; RFR = Risk Free Rate; TY = Terminal Year; OOCF = Organic Operating Cash Flow.

systematically exceeded which is the goal of any good management team.

Based on a robust valuation process, a company can identify its fair value corridor and regularly assess its position in it. If a company finds itself outside its fair value corridor or poised to be so, alarm bells should sound in the head of management. As we have discussed, acknowledgement of overvaluation is often shrugged off – "we deserve it" – and feelings of under-valuation are often not substantiated sufficiently robustly to convince shareholders. On the basis of this knowledge, management will be in a far better position to take a more active stand in driving and steering the valuation ascribed to the company and, equally significantly, establishing realistic valuation parameters which are sustainable in at least the medium term.

Management often deny they guide analyst valuations when in practice they do precisely that. Within the bounds of fiduciary care, this implicit management process needs to be founded on solid management insight and analysis and not left to any prevailing market bias.

The core determinants of effective self-valuation are the robustness of divisional forecasting and linking the valuation process to existing budgeting processes. This means that care and resource have to be applied to the process which in turn implies investment in people who can do it. Making decisions on divisional cashflow, discount rates and risk is more than something an IR director can do in their spare time. They need to be plugged into the budgeting round and given support to manage the model. Fair value therefore presupposes the integration of the budgeting and valuation processes and an integrated approach to the valuation process. As a consequence, the fair value measurement process has important implications for management structure and process which I will cover in detail in Chapter 12.

But, what should management do once they have understood their value position? If they cannot act on it, then the investment in measuring value is wasted. This is the position that a number of companies we interviewed found themselves in who had invested in valuation processes. Answering the question of "so what?" is where we go next.

6

Targeting value-determining investors

Identifying the shareholders that matter

THE VALUATION PROCESS IS A DIAGNOSTIC EXERCISE which can tell management when there is a problem with investor perceptions of the company or when there is likely to be an imminent problem as they cross the cusp of the fair value corridor. What it cannot tell management is what is causing that problem. Answering the "why?" begins with an understanding of a company's institutional investors. For it is they, or a subset of them, who will have set the market price.

Management typically have an intense but slightly wary relationship with institutional fund managers. The average large company has around 30 to 40 institutional holders of their stock, accounting for between 60% and 90% of their shares. In some instances there will be one or two large, active fund managers who will maintain an open and engaged dialogue with management, exerting their influence to get what they see as performance. These may include large

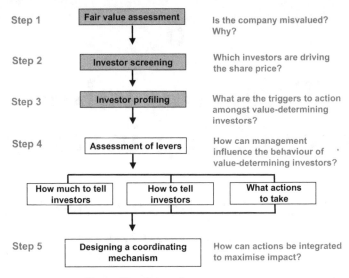

Figure 6.1 Fair value assessment.

family office funds. But, broadly speaking, management will tend to treat all fund managers alike. They will of course apportion more attention to those funds holding more than 2–3% of the shares, meaning two to three meetings with large holders per year. They will also typically meet with smaller institutional holders and respond to any requests they may make.

The challenge management faces is knowing which of these 30 to 40 fund managers is currently or is likely in the future to drive the shareprice and for what reasons. Even if management were to ask each fund manager outright how active a strategy they are pursuing and what their stock selection criteria are, they will rarely get clear answers. And they often don't even ask the question in the first place. The dominant characteristic of the average large-cap fund manager is, quite appropriately, obfuscation of motive and secrecy of action. Beyond generic attributions, such as style (growth, value, momentum, etc.) and broad risk profile, most large-cap fund managers will be opaque about their weighting intentions and their portfolio strategy.

Most fund managers will have endeavoured to remain below 3% of shares in issue, the level at which they are forced to disclose their holding. They will often also hold their shares through a proxy and certainly trade through a range of proxies, enabling them to retain greater trading flexibility, but in the process further obfuscating their actions. For many of these fund managers, the holding will reflect a sectoral index weighting as much as it will any fundamental views on the value of the company. They may have exercised some discretion about which two or three players to favour within a particular sector, but if they are focused on large-cap stocks they may have a very limited set of companies from which to choose. Individual company weightings will usually relate primarily to the index weighting of these companies in their sector. It is usually hard for an outside observer to evaluate the performance of a particular fund and near-on impossible to glean insights about the structure of the mandate underlying it. Meetings with fund managers are often not clear and hours can be invested with a feeling that there is a "relationship" when in reality there may be none.

During the course of our research, a number of CEOs and CFOs of large companies claimed a good personal "feel" for the core fund managers in their stock. They typically met each such fund manager twice a year, and their head of investor relations had regular contact with the buy-side analyst team assisting the fund manager. There often appeared to be an implicit belief on the part of the CEO that these things are about relationships and that they were the best positioned of anyone to get a handle on what the fund managers were thinking. The house broker monitored trading activity, but tying trading activity to fundamental insights about fund manager behaviour was quite rightly perceived as difficult and they often admitted that they rarely bother to do it. The process of investor management appeared to be conducted by touch and feel as much as anything else.

Management may express confidence that they have a "feel" for their shareholders, but how reliable is it really? The evidence of our research, combined with the clear volatility of so many stocks, suggests that it is not very reliable. The lack of reliability of personal "feel" helps explain why so many managers claim to feel "let down" or "misunderstood" by their investors. The net effect is that some large companies may have little real ability to differentiate between fund managers based on an understanding of motive and behaviour, except in the case of particularly large and active holders. This clearly holds its risks. How do you know how different investors will respond to changes in performance, to changes in the competitive environment or in the market at large?

That management should find it hard to predict the behaviour of their investors is hardly surprising. Despite their willingness to meet with management and listen to tales of strategy and derring-do, many large-cap fund managers are essentially passive. As we have explored, the dominance of tracker and closet index strategies means a growing swathe of fund managers have no fundamental interest in cherry-picking individual companies. Since many are closet indexers of one variety or another, it is understandable that they find it inappropriate to disclose this to management should they meet as part of a going-through-the-motions process with investee companies.

Even with active funds there is the issue of the fund manager's willingness and capacity to delve into the twists and turns of individual company research. The average large-cap investment manager oversees up to six portfolios, each containing around 85–100 stocks. As fund management companies come under pressure to lower costs and increase scale, so this "leverage ratio" of individual fund managers across portfolios is likely to grow. As a result, the bandwidth available to an individual fund manager to steep themselves in an individual company's strategy must logically be even more limited.

Even for those managers who are active and interested, the depth of knowledge of individual companies they are able to absorb, given these constraints, may not be vast. It would appear that some tend to confine their monitoring of individual companies to a "crib sheet" of around five or so data points which will vary company by company. In meeting with management, they are likely to be judging what they hear against these criteria; criteria of which they may not make management aware. It may only be in a relatively small number of instances that they will actively engage with management to understand the strategy and to propose where it might be deficient from their perspective.

This all poses a real challenge for management. Who is driving the shareprice and where should management focus their energies at any point in time? By default they often appear to spread their time and resources across the entire institutional investor base. This may explain why they spend up to a quarter of their time on investor issues. There are a lot of meetings to pack in and calls to make. The resulting communications process is effectively generic, based around a core presentation pack and underpinned by results presentations. Is this really the best way to address situations of misvaluation when the company finds itself outside the fair value corridor?

The minority matter

Treating all institutional investors alike and basing judgements on "feel" rather than analysis holds serious dangers for management. For most registers, it is the trading activity of a very small number of fund managers which causes major movements in the shareprice. During a given period of time, say 3 months, it is likely to be the same two or three fund managers who will drive trading direction in a particular stock. Often it is not easy to spot this phenomenon as the activity surrounding most company's shares is mired in "noise" created by trading momentum. There will also be the habitual buying and selling as funds adjust their weightings, trades related to hedge strategies, larger retail adjustments by private client funds, funds making trades related to the maturity of a mandate. Spotting a trend may well be possible based on simple eyeballing, but pinning it on particular protagonists is not easy. In some cases there will be some dominant and highly active fund which will have made itself and its objectives well known to management. In this case the identification task is done. But sometimes these critical fund managers may not be the most prominent or obvious investors on the share register and any motive they have may be unknown to management. This is perhaps why few companies appear to actively analyse the root dynamics of their share registers.

Our research confirms what a number of academics and consultants have observed – that it is the trading activity of a relatively small number of institutional fund managers in any stock that will account for the directional movement in its shareprice. In the case of a company with say 40 institutional holders, this may amount to 2–3 fund managers. Although these fund managers may hold less than, say, 5% of the company's shares between them, the trades of these fund managers will have a high level of influence on the shareprice.

This happens for two primary reasons. First, as many large-cap fund managers are closet indexers (i.e., ostensibly trackers, but more sensitive to pricing signals than pure trackers), they will often follow the movement in a particular stock of lead active investors. They will quickly establish who these leaders are and respond to their activity. In some cases, knowing who the leaders are will be general knowledge. The fund management industry is a relatively small one, there is a lot of migration of professionals between funds and plenty of "jungle drums" beating. The broker community is also a conduit for information. In other cases, who the leaders are may very much be a closely guarded secret by those in the know. Some followers may even engage in keeping an eye on the reaction of lead investors in analysts' meetings or at the AGM.

The second reason for the heavy influence of this minority will be the natural momentum of index investing. As a couple of active investors sell or buy, followed by a clutch of quicker moving closet indexers, so the company's position in the sector index will move and other purely passive fund managers will adjust their weightings accordingly. This then tends to be compounded by the activity of retail investors who tend to pick up on such trends last. The result can be dramatic movements in shareprice on the back of what can appear fairly marginal trades. I have already cited the infamous Rentokil example of this phenomenon.

Whilst in the case of Rentokil the reasons were clear – the loss of its 20% growth trajectory – in many cases management are left scratching their heads. How could the market over-react this way? How could they misinterpret us so badly? A typical reaction is to pour energy into tackling general market "sentiment", to boost communication of strategy, and to hold hard-hitting analyst meetings to stoke the PR machine. This when the root cause is the activity of two or three fund managers whose actions may not even relate to the company's strategy at all. In so reacting, it is possible management may create a problem that didn't really exist.

The fact that shareprices are set at the margin by a small subset of the investor base means that identifying these lead

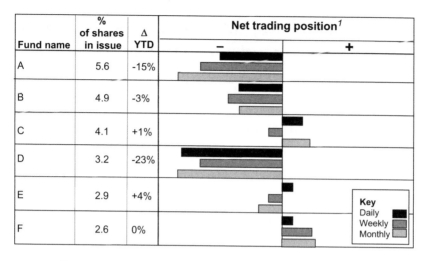

Fund name	% of shares in issue	Δ YTD	Net trading position[1] −	+
A	5.6	-15%		
B	4.9	-3%		
C	4.1	+1%		
D	3.2	-23%		
E	2.9	+4%		
F	2.6	0%		

Figure 6.2   Generic summary of shareholder movements.
[1] Net shares traded (Purchases − Sales).

investors and determining what drives their trading behaviour is critical to addressing misvaluation. On the whole, companies do not do this systematically. First, it is not always accepted that it is a subset of the register that has to be targeted when all instincts (and regulations) are driven to treating all investors alike. Second, there is often no analytical process to identify this active trading group. The existing best practice we identified in this regard was the sort of analysis illustrated in Figure 6.2. But, often this was not conducted with sufficient regularity to be useful. Nor does it identify the impact of the trading of these investors.

Given the funds in question will change over time, the process of identification is a particular challenge. Information the company controls about investors is often highly personalised and not codified. The basic material necessary to identify the funds in question is often lacking. Most companies will conduct an annual audit of their investors, polling opinion on a range of management issues, but this is unlikely to lead to great insight into who will drive their shareprice in the coming months.

As I have already mentioned, by default there is typically great reliance on the broker. The house broker may well be exposed to certain fund manager's activities across a number of companies and therefore observe their behaviour across a range of investments. But, whether they turn this into useful information for management of the particular company in question is another matter. It may not, in some circumstances, be in their interests to do so, particularly when the broker is primarily interested in keeping the fund manager's trading business and reserving their goodwill for an upcoming placing by another client. So, what should management do to seize control of this issue? That's where we go next.

Identifying value-determining investors

Those investors that set and drive the shareprice of companies I call "value-determining investors", meaning that they effectively set the value attached to the company. A value-determining investor is likely to have four characteristics:

- A material holding, probably greater than 1% of the company's shares.

- An active mandate from the provider of funds.

- The holding in the company in question is likely to represent greater than 3% of their portfolio, in other words a significant piece of the whole.

- They will probably be known to have a value-oriented style.

But, even these broad generalisations will not always hold true and help identify the funds in question. As we have discussed, appearances can be very deceptive in the fund management game. A value-determining investor may, for example, be a hedge fund seeking an arbitrage between a cyclical and a counter-cyclical sector. As soon as the cycle is fulfilled they may trade out. The only certainty is that trading activity by these holders will have coincided with material movements in the shareprice.

At the core of a fair value strategy is a systematic approach to identifying value-determining investors. On the basis of our research, and with reference to existing methodologies, we have articulated a simple approach to value-determining investor screening.[1] The objective of the screen is to determine when the trading activity of fund managers has coincided with unique and sustained movements in the shareprice. One dimension of the screen requires identifying instances when the shareprice of the company has suffered a material movement that cannot be attributed to sector or general market movements and which is therefore specific to the company. A material movement is typically one that is greater than 2.5% out of sync with the index. This means

[1] See Coyne and Witter, *McKinsey Quarterly* (2002b).

that the index will, for instance, have fallen 1%, but the company's shares will have fallen 3.5%. Deciding which index to use – whether sectoral, national or depending on the company, international – is clearly an important decision.

The other aspect of the material movement that is critical is that it is one that is not immediately reversed in the following number of trading days. A company's shares may suffer a one-time fall as a single fund sells down its holding, for example, because of liquidity issues in the fund. Provided these shares are picked up and the price stabilises again, then this will not be a value-determining event. So, for instance, if the company's shares fall 3% against a backdrop of stable sector and market indices, and this fall is not reversed over the following 5 trading days (e.g., it is not simply a blip), then the movement is unique and material. Such analysis will isolate movements when activity by certain holders has driven the price rather than general market movements influenced by the vagaries of unpredictable action by anonymous players. Such analysis is not trivial. It requires a good feel for the data. It requires a decision as to which index is appropriate. It also requires a decision as to the regularity of the analysis – weekly, monthly or some other period. All will influence the usefulness of the data.

The next question is: Which fund manager's trading activity appears to have coincided with these unique differential movements? To work this out it is necessary to estimate the net change in holdings amongst each of the institutional holders of the stock during the period in question. Like many things in investor strategy, calculating the net changes in holdings for institutional holders is not straightforward, as many will be trading through proxies and many will also be using derivatives rather than trading underlying shares (e.g., shorting and going long). Although potentially tortuous, both can ultimately be traced to their final holders through careful analysis of the register, probably with some assistance from the broker. A viable approach to the calculation of net changes in individual holdings is as follows:

(Purchases + Repayment of any borrowed shares)

– (Sales + Share borrowings)

Correlating these net changes in holdings against unique movements in shareprice whilst ensuring both relate to the same specific period (e.g., 1 week) should identify clearly which fund trades have been associated with unique movements in shareprice (Figure 6.3). No correlation analysis can guarantee cause and effect. One weakness with this analysis is that it is likely to capture both leaders but also a number of

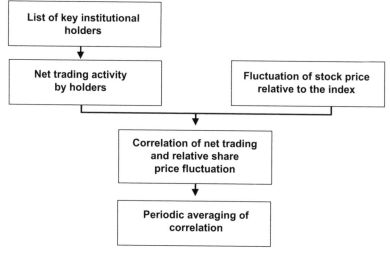

Figure 6.3 Basic investor-screening method.

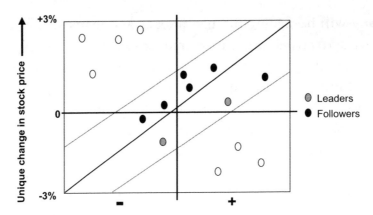

Figure 6.4 Net trading position amongst large institutional shareholders.

the quicker followers. In other words, whilst it will reduce the long list of potential funds to a shorter list, the list may not be short enough to be immediately helpful (Figure 6.4). The more regularly the analysis is performed and the shorter the intervals (e.g., weeks rather than months), the more possible it will be to identify patterns that winnow out value-determining investors. This presupposes that the company organises its own regular analysis rather than treating it as a one-off exercise, typically administered by an external consultant.

In many cases, value-determining investor analysis is likely to confirm management suspicions – *"I knew it was them, and now we have it in black and white."* But, as single snap-shots, it can be hard to be sure you are focusing on value-determining investors rather than rapid followers. However, performing this analysis on a monthly basis, and averaging outputs, should help build up a robust picture of value-determining investors v. followers in the stock (Table 6.1). Suddenly, management can begin to focus attention where

Table 6.1 Identifying value-determining investors

	Name of value-determining investors	% correlation with unique movement in shareprice[1]
January	A	72
	B	63
February	C	63
	B	81
	D	92
March	A	71
	B	69
April	D	62
	E	71
May	A	61
	B	78
June	A	82
	B	76
July	A	87
	D	69

[1] Measured as R^2.

it matters and speak to individual fund managers with conviction and insight.

The degree to which the company can hone its skills at performing this type of analysis will be critical to its value. In today's volatile markets the amount of general noise is high and the speed with which active investors move is also high. This is true in particular of hedge funds. This means that occasional analysis of the register will not yield useful information. To be effective, it has to be thorough and systematic so that the company can establish the normative behaviour of its investors.

Of course, identifying value-determining investors alone does not solve the misvaluation problem. Identification has to be complemented with an understanding of these fund managers' motives and behaviours. Without understanding these things, management will not be equipped to influence them. That's where we go next.

7

Profiling value-determining investors

Getting to know the culprits

IDENTIFYING THE VALUE-DETERMINING INVESTORS THAT may be driving the shareprice is only the first step towards managing the relationship with them. In order to attempt to influence their perceptions of the company, it is essential to understand the behaviour of these fund managers in order to predict how they will continue to behave. It may turn out that their strategy has nothing to do with perceptions of the company at all, or it may transpire they fundamentally disagree with a new approach taken by the company. Distinguishing between such motivations and behaviours is central to a fair value strategy.

Understanding behaviours is something more familiar to marketing people than finance people. But at the end of every institution is an individual fund manager driven by ambitions, fears as well as strategy. Few companies have a systematic procedure for profiling their core institutional investors. Often the management of a company will have been exposed to a lot of insight into their investors from various meetings, interactions or tip-offs from brokers. Such information gleaned from meetings, anecdotes and observations usually resides solely in the heads of two or three senior managers. The challenge is synthesising this information so that coherent judgements can be made from it. Often, important insights about particular fund managers can emerge from unexpected places, and never get absorbed and acted upon. The opportunities to coalesce and exchange that informal information may simply not crop up. It was a similar observation about the nature of corporate information in general that gave rise to the knowledge management movement. In the lingo of the knowledge management fraternity, the challenge is to turn "tacit" information residing in individual's heads into "institutionalised", managed information.

In the case of information regarding value-determining investors, the same issue is utterly critical. If you ask an Investor Relations (IR) director or a CFO for a clear, substantiated view of the motivation of a particular fund manager you will not always get a convincing answer. You will often get a feeling, a suspicion but not always a balanced verdict that could be the basis for action. The challenge of piecing together the pieces of insight is very much like building a mosaic.

Understanding value-determining investors is best thought of as an account management process. At the heart of the account management process is a profiling database. This is the formal framework for coalescing all the fragments of insight on individual fund managers. This needs to be regularly updated with titbits and insights, until a compre-

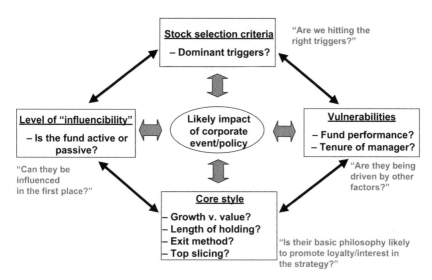

Figure 7.1 Basic investor profiling.

hensive profile emerges of each potential value-determining investor. The fair-value-profiling methodology we have developed on the basis of our research proposes that information about particular fund managers and their funds be organised into four categories (Figure 7.1):

- *Level of influencibility.* For example: Is there a reason to believe that the fund manager can actually be influenced or are they just a closet indexer? Do marginal active portfolio decisions get regularly made on the basis of debriefs and new information about the company? Or does the fund manager appear to be subject to across-the-board weighting decisions out of their control? What evidence has there been about their level of engagement with the company's strategy? Is this known to be an important investment for them? How long have they held the shares? A low level of engagement and significance, combined with unresponsiveness may point to the fact that the investment is part of an index strategy, in which case time spent on trying to influence them may be better employed elsewhere.

- *Core style*. For example: What is the fund manager's dominant style – value, growth, momentum or another? How long do they usually hold a stock and how long have they held ours? Are we at the cusp of their usual length of hold? How do they typically exit a position, "blast" or "bleed"? Do they tend to "top slice" or are they relatively inactive? Do they have particular sector biases? If the apparent fit between the strategy of the fund and that of the company is poor, then it may be a good clue to expect trouble. This is particularly so when the strategy of either the company or fund changes (e.g., from value to growth).

- *Vulnerabilities*. For example: Has the fund's performance been below its peer group? Is there any insight into the length and security of the fund's mandates? Is the individual manager under pressure or likely to be changed altogether? What benchmarks does the fund appear to be measured against? Does the fund appear to be too concentrated in this sector or indeed a particular share? Vulnerabilities will give good clues to possible instability. Often, these vulnerabilities give rise to trading that can be entirely unrelated to the company's performance or prospects.

- *Investment triggers*. For example: How does the fund manager track individual stocks and what are his or her responses to generic triggers such as buy-backs, M&A, change of executives, etc? Is there a history of strong response to half-year performance to forecast? What peer group are they measuring us against? Is there any clear pattern to their trading activity?

Building up profile sheets on key value-determining investors is essential to engaging with them properly. This means that management attention is focused on those investors that matter and their likely triggers to action can be factored into the planning round. The company can build up individual profiles (Table 7.1) and then consolidate these into a composite sheet (Table 7.2) in order to get a sense of relative vulnerability and hence priorities. These forms can be

Table 7.1 Example of basic investor profiling

Fund A	Key characteristic	Status
Level of influencibility	Index orientation	Low
	Significance of holding to portfolio	High
	Level of company consultation	High
	Holding horizon	Long
Vulnerabilities	Performance of fund	Good
	Tenure of manager	4 years
	Maturity of mandate, if any	Unknown
	Level of fund concentration	Unknown
Core style	Value orientation	High
	Growth orientation	Medium
	Rotation	Low
	Sector bias	High
Known investment triggers	Management change	High
	Acquisition	Low
	Dividend change	Low
	Buy-back programme	Low

Table 7.2 Basic investor profiling

Fund name	Level of influencibility	Vulnerabilities	Fit of core style[1]	Fit of known investment triggers[2]	Summary status of relationship	Fund-specific action points
A	High	Low	High	High	Strong	None
B	Low	Unknown	Low	Low	Weak	Substitute
C	Medium	Moderate	Moderate	Moderate	Questionable	Address actively
D	High	Low	High	High	Strong	None
E	Medium	High	Moderate	Moderate	Questionable	Needs work
F	High	Low	High	High	Strong	None
G	Unknown	Unknown	Unknown	Unknown	Medium	Needs research

[1] Degree to which fund manager style fits with corporate strategy.
[2] Degree to which fund manager triggers suit likely behaviour of company.

managed on a PC and will underpin the account management process.

Coopting value-determining investors

Once a level of understanding is achieved about value-determining investors, the next logical step is to engage with them more fully to respond to their objectives and enter into a dialogue about how the company can help them fulfil these. The reality, of course, is there will be those fund managers who it turns out are value-determining but have no fundamental interest in the company. These might include hedge funds. I will talk about what a company can do about the relationship with these in a moment. If asked to contribute, a number of mainstream large-cap fund managers may turn around and throw their hands up – *"Look, this isn't my job. That's what you get paid to do. Don't ask us about strategy. Just deliver on your promises."*

With a typical large-cap fund manager unable to devote more than 6 hours per year to each stock in their portfolio, this is all hardly surprising. That translates into perhaps two meetings with management per year, half a dozen phone calls and a handful of sessions with the buy-side analyst, and perhaps a cursory review of the sell-side analyst notes every few months. That is not the sort of time commitment conducive to inputting into the strategy process of an investee company. Combine that with the fact that the average tenure for a fund manager is 3 years, and the usual period over which their performance-based compensation matures is at most 2 years, and you have a recipe for probably mild disinterest in management's overtures.

Then there will be those fund managers who are receptive to dialogue which in itself is not always a straightforward proposition for management. One implication of the fair value process is that management may have to get closer to investors who they feel are "thorns in their sides" – the agitators who hone in on board issues. This can be extremely uncomfortable. Management instinct is usually to shy away from allowing individual fund managers to get too interventionist and dominant. The most "comfortable" register is one where no fund holds more than 3% of issued shares, and fund managers are relatively disengaged, particularly when it comes to vetting remuneration packages. But, a fair value strategy requires a very different attitude towards value-determining fund managers who are willing to be engaged with.

Our research suggests that companies which manage to get themselves back in the fair value corridor from a position of undervaluation tend to actively coopt one or two active investors to underwrite their strategy. These are typically large, active holders for whom the investment is significant and who believe management have a sound value strategy that needs time and support to deliver. Coopting a fund manager means consulting with them closely, even to the point of making them a temporary "insider". Being prepared to be coopted is a major decision for a fund manager because it effectively locks them into an illiquid position, as they will probably be prohibited from trading by stock exchange rules whilst they are privy to such management insight. It is also a big and often counter-intuitive decision for management. As a result, there are few fund managers and few companies who actively engage in aligning their interests so closely, even if funds such as Hermes Focus have demonstrated it to be a potentially powerful strategy.

Most well-run businesses do not find themselves in the position of having to coopt lead investors to underpin an otherwise shaky register. It is usually more a matter of honing and fine-tuning from within the fair value corridor. But even this can unlock great value. The core of a fair value strategy lies in the dialogue with value-determining investors. This is not always easy. The ability to engage these funds with the strategy and longer term potential of the businesses will determine how well management succeed in keeping the company inside the fair value corridor.

The substitution game

Of course, one possible outcome of the screening and profiling process may be that certain value-determining investors have a fundamental disinterest in the company, a poor fit with the company's strategy or otherwise pose a real threat to the stability of its register because of their unpredictability. Hedge funds and a variety of special situation funds sometimes fall into this camp. One clear possibility is that management should proactively seek to substitute out that investor or at least prepare one or a number of better suited investors to step into the breach when the inevitable large block trades occur. This sounds all very logical and simple but, as any IR director will know, in practice it is far from simple.

For a start, since many companies do not screen for value-determining investors and then profile them, they may have little idea who would be a candidate for proactive substitution. Few value-determining investors will put their hands up and admit to constituting an overhang in the stock. Hopefully this book has made a small contribution to rectifying that challenge. For the company which has identified its less aligned value-determining investors, the next problem is how and where should substitute funds be found?

One common method used to find substitutes is to conduct competitor share register analysis. This involves identifying those funds that have invested to certain weightings in competitor firms in the sector but not invested in our firm (as they presumably like the sector). These fund managers might potentially be persuaded to shift their sector bets a little more evenly. Alternatively, there will be those funds which invest in similar profile businesses in other sectors but which are entirely absent from this particular sector altogether. These fund managers may be persuaded of the wisdom of some sector exposure to round out their portfolio.

The company typically turns to the house broker to perform this type of analysis, as they will have better data about the fund management community than the company. Once again, over-reliance on this source of help runs the risk of moving the company away from its fair value mission, as it will no longer be actively managing the alignment between the company's strategy and its institutional investors. The more opportunity the company has to identify, understand and attempt to influence its value-determining investors, the better positioned it will be to know ahead of time when substitution would be desirable and what sort of fund might constitute an appropriate substitute. The sort of substitute analysis I have outlined above, as simple as it is, is about as systematic as some brokers get anyhow. Again, it is a competence well worth developing in-house.

In summary . . .

The fair value process we have gone through in the last three chapters – from valuation, through to identification, to profiling – is not an easy one. It demands that the company take a proactive stance in interpreting how fund managers influence its shares and how they might act in the future. It demands that management take a firm hand in developing an internal valuation model to guide their management of sell-side analysts. It demands that they screen their register regularly for the activity of value-determining investors. It demands that they apply a rigorous profiling methodology in order to predict investor behaviour. This all means investment and resources. The average direct costs of the IR function probably amount to something around £2–£3m for the average FTSE company, which includes broker retainers, annual report costs, venues for AGMs, as well as salaries for the IR team. The indirect costs of executive management time are probably even higher. To pursue a fair value strategy, direct costs are likely to increase and ideally indirect costs should decrease. But, still, the investment in information and systems will be material.

Clearly, this would all be little more than a futile academic exercise if, as a result of this improved information, the company were not able to act on it to change the behaviour of its key investors – meaning quite simply encouraging a seller or potential seller to become a holder or even a buyer within the strictures of fair value principles. The ultimate challenge of changing investor perceptions and behaviour is where we go next.

Part Three

Delivering a Fair Value Strategy

8

Towards fair value levers

Knowing a good lever from a bad lever

IF YOU'VE BEEN STALWART ENOUGH TO MAKE IT THIS FAR through the book, you will appreciate we have covered a lot of terrain, through from the valuation process, to identifying value-determining investors, to attempting to understand their motivations and behaviours. The ultimate challenge is attempting to influence their perceptions and behaviours. At the core of the challenge of influencing investor perceptions is how we set their expectations – in other words, what they expect from us in terms of future performance. If we do not set expectations correctly in the first place, our ability to fine-tune our interaction with them will be largely gone. Getting the expectation-setting process right is the precursor to influencing perceptions and behaviour. The simple objective of all management teams should be delighting shareholders by exceeding expectations. In many companies, the setting of expectations is a process mired in obscurity and skulduggery. Above all, it does not appear to help reduce misvaluation,

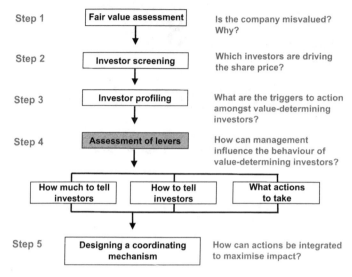

Figure 8.1   Fair value assessment.

often creating expectations that cannot be met, let alone exceeded.

The expectation-setting process in most companies is uniquely focused on half-year and full-year performance. That is where 90% of energy is typically invested both by management and analysts. Management are, of course, prohibited from providing forecast information directly to investors. Rather, this job falls to sell-side analysts who tease it out through their superior knowledge of the company. In reality, it will have been arrived at through a highly con-sultative process. A lead analyst will be nudged towards what management feel is an attainable, tightly banded range of half- and full-year outcomes. They will typically centre on revenue growth, operating margins, profits after tax and earnings per share. Other lesser analysts will usually follow the lead analyst's predictions because they will recognise that these individuals have better quality access to the company and therefore better insight. This is partly why analysts' forecasts tend to cluster in a tight band.

The management team then in effect signs up to the forecast given by the analyst and broker through a series of meetings with the broad constituency of analysts following the company. This then becomes the "market consensus". It can all be a bit of a matter of wink and nudge which gives all the players a partial but far from complete "out" if the forecast should prove slightly wrong. A major miss will of course be met with shareholder fury.

The forecasting process as it stands suits the objectives of the house broker and lead analyst. It gives them a hold over the company which in turn gives them transactional access. Without playing such a core role in the forecasting round, their ability to generate commissions as primary market maker or to secure corporate finance mandates would be more limited. In some cases it is probable that their primary instinct is to build expectations and to see a rise in shareprice which suits all stakeholders.

As a result, the instincts of the house broker are sometimes to push for as aggressive a full-year forecast as possible, in turn driving transactional activity for the brokerage. Management often actively support this as they can see the impact on shareprice, even if the forecast given is somewhat out of whack with the internal budget. Often, any discrepancy is fuzzy because companies typically run an internal stretch budget which is above market expectations anyway. However, such budgets are also typically scaled back during the course of the year, potentially creating a real gap between actual deliverable performance and market expectations. It is bridging this gap that causes so much heart-ache at year end and which sometimes gives rise to recourse to the box of accounting tricks.

Performance against annual expectations is something investors take very seriously. If an annual "forecast" is missed by a material margin – say, in excess of 10% – then it is likely that the stock will be marked down by 20–30%. Most stocks suffer value erosion at a rate that is a multiple of their annual profit erosion, reflecting their PE ratio. The loss of value is usually built in before the final full-year number is delivered, through a process of whispers and, if it really looks bad, formal profit warnings – heads-up given to the market that full-year expectations are likely not to be met. If disappointing numbers are announced without prior warning, then value erosion can be much more severe. ARM, the UK's leading designer of microchips outperformed the average IT stock by 60% until late 2002. Then, a week before the announcement of its interim results, it issued a profits warning. Its stock fell almost 30% over 5 days before stabilising.

The profit-warning procedure is a critical component of the expectation management process in periods of undeliverable expectations, where the risks of negative over-reaction are very real. The main objective of the profit-warning process is to act as an escape valve – to slowly deflate expectations and attempt to avoid a stark correction in stock value. Only 25% of first profit warnings are not then followed by at least one further warning in the next 12-month period. By the third warning most stocks will typically have shed half their value. As the earnings warnings grow so the "rating" of the company also declines. If it started at a PE ratio of 16, by the time it gets to the third warning it may well be down at 10. If the declining PE ratio is applied to lowered earnings, you get a double whammy. This accounts for the increasingly dramatic decline in market capitalisation and stock price as forecasts persistently fail to be met. Our research suggests that once a company has been severely downwardly re-rated it takes an average of 7 years for it to recover its original rating. During this re-rating period many companies are effectively undervalued and hence the cost to shareholders is high.

Many large companies, burdened with raised expectations, go to great lengths to avoid resorting to profit warnings. Some avenues of escape are offered by resorting to accounting techniques to smooth earnings, such as management of provisions, revenue recognition and treatment of costs. This flurry of finessing usually springs to life around the half-year and then accelerates towards the end of the reporting year, as revenue recognition is accelerated, costs are pushed back and provisions are released. Often, this fundamentally distorts normal operating behaviour, driving changes of strategy, such as embarking on acquisitions to bolster short-term earnings, cutting capital expenditure to boost cashflow, hiving out costs into divestitures and a range of other wheezes. They all tend to be delaying rather than solving tactics.

What alternatives does management have to managing the books or risking profit warnings? This takes us back to the forecasting process and the setting of expectations. The real question is how does management avoid raising expectations beyond what they (management) can deliver? This may sound very banal and obvious but it appears from our research very hard for management to stick to. It is all too easy to get caught up in the expectation-raising game. A management team may recognise the dangers of over-promising and set a moderate target of expectations which it can reliably exceed. Once the team has done that for 2 years straight, the stock price will have inevitably responded favourably. By the end of the second year of consistent delivery above expectations, the stock is likely to become substantively re-rated. By the third year, what appeared at first to be a modest percentage growth in earnings, suddenly becomes a far greater absolute hurdle. Each half-year becomes an ever-growing mountain to achieve. All possible future outperformance is built into the stock price. There's only one way to go.

So, how is this expectations inflation trap avoided? Should the company opt out of the analysts' forecasting cycle as far as possible? Should it refuse to take their meetings? This is of course both unrealistic and also undesirable. The pressure on the firm to provide guidance is typically overwhelming. It is only giants such as Intel and Gillette and companies controlled by that greatest of value investors, Warren Buffett, that have attempted this. Even if a company should dare take that position, by default analysts will produce forecasts independently and it will not be clear to investors to what degree the company has tacitly signed up to them or not. There is a clear risk in the loss of control by the company. So, the analyst community is there to be managed, not bypassed.

Alternatively, should the company continually act to deflate expectations? The commonly perceived risk with this is that readjusting expectations downwards will itself cause the shareprice to fall and may even be interpreted as a fundamental profits warning. As a result, expectation adjustment typically occurs following a de-rating and the appointment of new management with a new strategy – the clean sweep approach. It is far more challenging to do in expectation of a problem as an incumbent management team.

A third potential path is to try to switch attention away from half- and full-year forecasts and instead focus on longer term value projections. After all, around 50–80% of any valuation lies in the perpetuity that is more than 5 years out. This, in principle, holds the promise of reducing the need to inflate short-term expectations. The notion of longer term value projections I call "the value story". Essentially, it is the communication of value drivers that support internal fair valuation. Shifting the focus from annual forecasts to the value story can be a viable expectation management strategy in certain circumstances. I will talk about this at length in Chapter 9.

A fourth potential path is to complement financial measures of performance with a variety of other measures that give greater insight into the value story and fair valuation. This amounts to setting objectives which are non-financial in nature but which provide clear indicators of future value. These might be a wide range of measures, from market share, customer acquisition, product ratings, brand recognition or a range of other measures of market impact. They might relate to productivity or scrap. They might even relate to measures of innovation. These non-financial measures would need to be shown to be better long-term indicators of future value creation than historical financial accounting measures. I will have much to say about this in Chapter 9, and plenty of work has been done on this by advisors such as PricewaterhouseCoopers.

Unfortunately for managers, it is a real battle to get the markets to take non-financial measures seriously. They are typically industry-specific, technical in nature and not strictly comparable across a portfolio. Hence, they can be largely irrelevant to the time-starved fund manager unless thought through robustly and well presented.

From what to how …

Having decided what to say, a management team also has to decide how to say it. Broadly speaking, the "how" divides into two areas – direct communication and indirect signalling. Within the two camps there is a multitude of possibilities. The direct path would in principle look a limited opportunity set against value-determining investors. Communication direct to fund managers of facts that are potentially impactful on shareprice is governed by clear laws of disclosure – they must be released to all shareholders at the same time. But, when it comes to qualitative interpretations, particularly into the future, then there is far more room for manoeuvre, as we will explore.

There have been suggestions from some quarters that the investor relations process could be viewed as a marketing event. But, that is wildly over-simplifying the motives of investors. Communications alone is a blunt tool. Rather

than relying solely on direct communications, most sophisticated management teams also make use of indirect
signalling devices, most commonly when the shareprice is
under pressure.

There is typically a hierarchy of signalling actions used to
defend the shareprice. First, the CEO or chairman puts
appropriate pressure on their fellow board members to buy
stock. A number of analytical services track director share
dealings and this is information followed by many fund managers. It is often interpreted by the financial press as signalling
that the company is undervalued. If the decline continues,
companies then typically resort to share buy-backs or
enhanced dividend programmes. Most companies have some
form of share buy-back programme. They hum along at a low
key, soaking up a residue of excess operating cash and, in
buying shares, reduce the denominator of the EPS calculation,
so enhancing earnings per share. Dividends, by contrast, are
viewed as long-term policy and structural in nature. If the
dividend is raised, then subsequently reduced, the stock is
typically punished. The benefit of the buy-back is that it is
viewed as an exceptional event and does not create an annual
expectation amongst investors to the same degree as a
dividend. But, correspondingly, it typically receives a less
favourable response than a dividend increase which signals
a commitment to increasing yield and potentially the shift
towards being an income stock. Indeed, share buy-backs can
drive a fall in shareprice if the signal received is that the
company no longer has growth opportunities in which to
invest. But, in general, the buy-back is the favoured weapon
to fight immediate shareprice erosion.

The problem with buy-backs and dividends is that their effect is typically short-lived and one-off. A number of empirical studies have shown that they do not alter the medium-term trajectory of a shareprice. Because most management teams have not thought through the alternative signalling actions they can take to effect expectations, they often resort to "action steps". In periods of downturn, corporate "action steps" usually mean focus and rationalisation. In other words, divesting "non-core" assets and streamlining the cost structure of core operations. Often, this translates into jettisoning many of the very operations added through acquisition in the upturn, typically with a material loss in underlying value to shareholders. In the case of companies that have swung from large premiums to discounts, the process of becoming rehabilitated often demands a change in the management team. That businesses and their corporate centres should follow the market cycle through expansion and contraction is hardly surprising. But, the damage to long-term strategy and value creation that can result means it is a far-from-optimal approach. Surely, there is a better way to manage expectations, particularly amongst value-determining investors?

In search of non-disruptive value levers

The objective of fair value strategy is to keep the business firmly in the fair value corridor. It is also designed to enable a company that has strayed outside the corridor to return as swiftly as possible. Fair value strategy is based on the use of a range of techniques to influence expectations amongst value-determining investors. These I call "value levers". Our research into companies that have remained in the fair value corridor, and those that have managed to return to it having left it, suggests there are a range of value levers available to management to condition expectations. Value levers can be grouped into three areas:

- *What we say* to investors, in other words what facts and interpretations do we disclose? What is the balance between annual forecasts and the value story (e.g., financial performance measures, operating measures, market indicators, strategic objectives, management quality, etc.)?

- *How we communicate,* using either direct channels or indirect signals? What is the best way to communicate targeted messages (e.g., use of buy-backs and dividends and other signalling devices, selection of different communications mediums, timing of announcements).

- *What actions we take* to stay in or return to the fair value corridor (e.g., changes to the non-exec board, remuneration policy, capital structure, strategy, etc.).

The relevance and appropriateness of different value levers will vary depending where the firm finds itself in its fair value corridor. For a company that finds itself outside the fair value corridor and deep in undervaluation, it may be inevitable that a change of strategy is the only signal that will cut ice. For a company that is beginning to drift outside the corridor, the judicious use of buy-backs, combined with a change of remuneration policy to reflect aggressive margin improvement goals, plus appointment of a vocal non-exec, may be sufficient to arrest the slide. For the company that finds itself 30% overvalued, focusing on managing short-term expectations may be what matters most.

Broadly speaking, levers can be divided into two types – those that demand serious disruption to how the company is currently run, either through exposing performance challenges, requiring a change of strategy, capital structure or indeed management. These I call "disruptive value levers" and are usually only resorted to when the company is heavily adrift. The other group of levers can be deployed within the context of an existing strategy and without requiring a change of management. These I call "non-disruptive value levers." The use of non-disruptive value levers to address misvaluation is clearly more palatable to management and is where this book will focus its attention.

By performing an analysis of the relationship between the trading activity of value-determining investors over the past year and the implementation of value levers, the company may be able to build up a clearer view of whether non-disruptive levers are likely to be sufficient in their own right or whether disruptive levers will ultimately be called for. Figure 8.2 illustrates the output of this sort of analysis. The assumption in this book is that most management teams would be wise to test out non-disruptive levers before disrupting strategy and management.

Before we look at each non-disruptive value lever in detail, it is worth making a few general points. Each of these non-

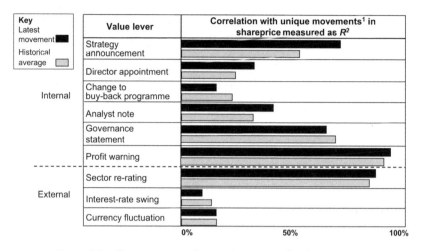

Figure 8.2 Illustrative analysis of impact of value levers.

[1] Unique movements are movement at least 2.5% differential from the index that are not reversed in the following 5 trading days.

disruptive value levers tends to fall under the management auspices of different teams within most corporate parents, ranging from the finance group to the strategy group. The evidence from our research suggests that the levers are most impactful when coordinated as part of an integrated strategy – a fair value strategy. One real problem is that in most large companies there is no integrating mechanism, and no single manager empowered to combine levers behind an investor strategy. This is an issue I will address in more detail in Chapter 12.

Another major point raised by these value levers is that few large companies appear to have a clear method for how to use them and how to measure their effect on value-determining investors. Indeed, in many cases they may not have acknowledged them as potential levers at all. They may not, for example, think of disclosure as a potential competitive weapon. Indeed, many of these levers tend to be regarded with suspicion and as undesirable. By default, many are only actually used when regulatory pressure demands it. A change of mindset is required whereby non-disruptive levers are viewed as a potential source of competitive advantage against the target group of value-determining investors.

Non-disruptive fair value levers are, in principle, suited to keeping a well-run business within the fair value corridor. If a company has slipped outside the corridor, then our research would suggest that disruptive levers may be necessary to return it to the corridor. A fair value strategy aims to avoid this eventuality. The next step in forming a clear view on what might constitute fair value levers for a particular company is to review each of the broad groups of generic non-disruptive fair value levers in turn, which is where we go next.

9

Deciding how much to tell investors

When ignorance is not bliss

PROPOSING THAT TELLING INVESTORS MORE ABOUT the company is a potential value lever may seem a counter-intuitive suggestion to some senior managers. Disclosure usually means trouble. It is deeply ingrained in the management psyche that the less that is disclosed, the more flexibility is created to avoid unpleasant surprises. This is particularly so around year ends when revenue is commonly accelerated, deals are consolidated and costs are deferred. It is central to many companies' strategies that earnings smoothing is a legitimate method of managing investor expectations, and reducing the amount that is told to investors facilitates that juggling act.

The company is in effect granted considerable leeway over how much it discloses and how the information is presented. If you asked a panel of CFOs their preferred option, a majority are likely to vote for reduced disclosure. The reason often given is that there is a fear of giving away sensitive information to the competition. The real reason is because the less that is disclosed the more discretion exists to manage reported performance – that an underperforming division can be cloaked by excessive (although perhaps unsustainable) performance from another division; the under-performing acquisition can evade scrutiny by avoiding separate disclosure; the excessive reliance on acquired revenues can be disguised by not separating out core from new clients beyond the year of the deal. A poor year can be redeemed by dragging revenues forward. Write-downs of over-valued assets can be carefully timed. Accruals can be reversed to redeem end-of-year shortfalls. The list is endless. The less disclosure the easier it is to hit the numbers expected by shareholders.

By default, demand for greater disclosure tends to come from the regulator. Our research suggests that, amongst FTSE 250 companies, after a 3-year period of intense pressure to increase disclosure, the average large company has only made between five and ten additional substantive disclosure points in their accounts beyond previous practice. Disclosure has historically been regulation-led, and not company-led.

Over a longer period of time companies in general have remorselessly disclosed ever more about themselves. This is largely in response to regular bouts of regulatory tightening by the stock exchange, FSA and their equivalents in other markets. But, companies have also got more sophisticated in explaining to investors and analysts the more fundamental drivers of value in the business. The average annual report by a FTSE 250 company has expanded from 42 pages in 1980 to around 68 pages in 2000. These are also now complemented

Figure 9.1 The company–fund manager relationship. What characteristics make for a good relationship between fund managers and management (% of respondents citing critical factor)?
Source: Adapted from IRS data (2002).

with elaborate websites. The reason large companies have begun gradually to overcome their instinctual distrust of disclosure is that they increasingly recognise it is an issue of competitive advantage.

Perhaps not surprisingly, the various regular surveys done of institutional fund managers show that the degree to which the company opens its kimono is an increasingly dominant driver of their confidence to invest (Figure 9.1). Similar research by one of the large accounting firms confirms the same findings – that the more a company says about itself, the more credibility will be conferred on it (Figure 9.2). As any seasoned finance director will tell you, such findings have to be taken with a pinch of salt. Most would argue that an effective strategy of earnings smoothing will do more to build investor trust than disclosure of the full ups and downs of the monthly earnings cycle. Within reason, you tell investors what they want to hear rather than what a forensic accountant would want to hear. Nevertheless, there is some evidence to support the notion that a company that is more frank about its value-generating capability than its immediate competitor, who sticks purely to the disclosure rules, will enjoy some sort of competitive advantage. Quantifying the size of the advantage has proved impossible, and

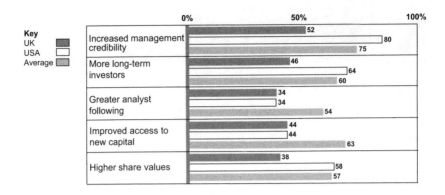

Figure 9.2   The benefits of full disclosure (% of respondents citing factor as a benefit of further disclosure).
Source: Adapted from PricewaterhouseCoopers.

there are many caveats that can be raised in particular situations.

Our research would suggest that strategies of shareprice maximisation tend to be associated with strategies of low disclosure and aggressive accounting treatment. In order to create and appear to satisfy ever-increasing expectations, share-value-maximising companies typically need all the flexibility they can muster to meet their numbers. The veil is thrown up. It is only logical that a strategy of fair value is likely to be underpinned by a philosophy of openness. But, it would be naive to suggest that increased disclosure *per se* will keep a company in the fair value corridor or indeed return it to the corridor. The question is where specifically can a company tell more that will influence the perceptions of value-determining investors in particular? How can management work out where the opportunities lie, and where the pitfalls lurk?

Dishing out more numbers ...

The character of managements' and also investors' approach to what is and is not disclosed has its roots in the accounting process. The accounting process has in part created a mindset of minimising what is said to the regulatory minimum and managing what is said to fit expectations. Post Enron and WorldCom, everyone has now woken up to the fact that accountancy is not a science, it's an art. It leaves plenty of room for liberal interpretation, for dubious application and endless revision. How do you value goodwill? When is revenue revenue? When are costs exceptional v. recurring? When can a cost be capitalised? What is the real value of assets on the balance sheet, such as buildings and machinery? When can a provision be released? The list is endless and on each line item of the P&L, balance sheet and cashflow statement there is room for ambiguity. Into this vacuum enters discretion.

Companies often quite naturally treat accounting just like any of us treat laws in general – we obey the spirit, but we often push the boundaries. Driving consistently 10 m.p.h. over the speed limit we are technically breaking the law, but it doesn't feel like we are committing a high felony. Pushing accounting rules can feel just the same. It is a matter of pushing the boundaries in order to deliver the number that is expected. The policeman in this self-policing system is the auditor who is fundamentally compromised as regulator. The oft-repeated theatrical scene is the accountancy partner having to negotiate with the FD over what is disclosed in the accounts. At the same time they will be having to negotiate the audit fee. One hat will say "it is my job to make sure they don't pull the wool over readers eyes," another will be "we'd better not irritate them so much they threaten to switch the account." Indeed, most accountancy firms acknowledge earnings smoothing to be a legitimate strategy by management to manage expectations and interpretation of performance.

Does this present any real issue for a company pursuing a strategy of fair value? Surely, such flexibility in the accounting system means the smart company can use deepened disclosure to its advantage? In principle, this argument makes sense, but, in practice, the fungible nature of accounting offers a real temptation for the company looking to maximise its shareprice. Earnings smoothing quickly turns into a desperate scrabble to meet raised annual forecasts, and with each year the hurdle consequently gets higher.

The other fundamental flaw with the accounting and audit process is that it is all retrospective. It examines the past and attempts to present it as neatly and succinctly as possible in prescribed line items. As we have discussed, all that matters for the institutional investor is the future, as this is what will create value. The same is true of management trying to work out the size of their fair value corridor and the position of the company in it. History is a guide to the future but not a perfect one. By the time the accountants sign off on the numbers, investor pricing decisions have usually been made. Things will have moved on. If there is a gap between expectations and actual outcomes this will have been dealt with through the profit-warning process long before the accounts are published. What investors crave is exactly what the published accounts cannot give them – an insight into the future.

Managers are quite familiar with gleaning insights into the future. They have to do so to create their budget and plan capacity. In part, budgets are created based on simple growth from the historical base. But, they are almost always complemented by the use of more fundamental operating measures – customer retention, new revenue wins, pipeline products, production efficiency, brand recognition, staff capability – all those measures that give a real feel for the customer franchise and the strength of the business in its market place.

Accounting and disclosure regulations usually do not touch on most of these measures and, perhaps consequently, few companies make serious disclosure on operating measures and rarely in a way that can be reliably compared across companies for benchmarking purposes. The accountancy profession is pretty much silent on them also. There is also possibly a certain level of fund manager disinterest in such measures. They will tend to be sector- if not company-specific, somewhat technical in nature, based on measurement standards that are not familiar, and not always easy to relate back to cashflow. Given the average active fund manager has so little time, the focus is usually quite naturally on the basic financial measures, such as earnings per share (EPS), revenue growth and margins.

One effect of low disclosure is to reinforce the value added of sell-side analysts. In the absence of deep disclosure, the interpretations made by analysts of the accounts assume greater importance to institutional investors despite any biases in favour of optimism. The claim could also be made that the minimal disclosure mentality also contributes to the herd mentality of some institutional large-cap fund managers. Lack of insightful data on individual companies makes a closet index strategy all the more appealing. If you cannot get real insight except through fundamental, in-depth research, why bother at all? A single company perhaps, except for the likes of Vodafone, cannot possibly justify the time in terms of portfolio weighting. Following this logic, it is possible to relate low disclosure to many of the challenges of the institutional investor dynamic we have talked about.

Low disclosure has its costs . . .

A strategy of disclosure minimisation typically comes unstuck eventually. Mistrust sets in about the contribution of certain acquisitions. Doubt emerges about the quality of revenue. Questions are asked about reliability of accruals and cost accounting. Marketplace cracks begin to appear and may belie good historical financials. Low disclosure can often allow issues of revenue and profit growth to be pushed out for a year or two. But, the eventual release of detailed information, usually under pressure due to sustained under performance in the stock, then leads to a major loss of confidence. *"If they didn't tell us about that failing division till we asked, how can they be trusted with anything?"* The value impact of this type of event was evidenced by the temporary decline of Shell's shareprice following several disclosures of overstated reserves. The result of increased disclosure following a strategy of low disclosure is often correction. Incoming CEOs who inherit a flagging stock tend to "kitchen-sink" such information so that it is not attributed to them.

Institutional fund managers are not always blameless either. Attitudes by fund managers towards disclosure tend to follow the economic cycle. When stocks are booming everyone is happy just to bask in augmenting portfolio value without demanding more insight, particularly if indexed. When markets decline a larger section of investors will typically have far greater appetite for high levels of disclosure. This potentially accentuates the misvaluation cycle, as good times hide storm clouds and bad times expose worse to come.

Changing mindsets

So, within this context, how can telling more to shareholders help deliver a fair value strategy? The logical connection is quite obvious. One potential source of the discrepancy between management's perception of value and the value placed on the company by the market is information. Management often know, or at least they believe they know, what the market does not. In cases of overvaluation many management teams will typically deny this, and in times of undervaluation they will tend to strenuously agree. A company in pursuit of fair value will inherently be anxious to be understood as perfectly as possible to get itself firmly in the fair value corridor. It will want shareholders to see the potential of good assets and to acknowledge the poor potential of other assets. This implies something which is anathema to most FDs – full and total disclosure.

The logic to this argument is fairly incontrovertible – that the more complete the market knowledge the more accurate the valuation attributed to the company is likely to be. If investors are privy to profit and revenue performance down to the relevant division, or even SBU, by geography and product line, it would in principle be harder for them not to be able to form a clear view of value. Following fair value principles, it would also be harder for them to contest management's view of value.

But, however good the logic, it does not appear that way to many companies. There is a big hurdle to overcome. The depth of disclosure in many large public companies is surprisingly thin. Few companies reveal divisional data. Virtually no company breaks out SBU data, brand data or client data. Very few companies disclose an acquired company's performance separate from core organic performance beyond the year of acquisition. The lowest level of split, set by a mixture of peer pressure and best practice, tends to be by geography and major product category line (e.g., passenger vehicles v. trucks).

Without exception, all companies run two sets of parallel accounts – management accounts and audited accounts – or three if you include tax computations. Management accounts are used to run the company and audited accounts to tell the markets how the company is doing. The greater the discrepancy between the level of disclosure of the two sets of accounts, logically the greater the information divide. Currently, on average the divide often appears great indeed.

In addition, many companies also appear to offer limited insight into non-financial measures of performance that might be indicators of future profitability in the sector, such as industry developments, the evolving nature of competition, the threat posed by new entrants, the threat of substitute technology, the evolving barriers to entry or the power of suppliers. They also tend to be reluctant to disclose detailed internal operating measures. This might be as concrete as productivity yields or client retention rates. Or it might be as qualitative as staff morale and customer satisfaction ratings.

Whilst most management teams will give a flavour of industry developments and operating issues in their meetings with fund managers, there often appears to be a low level of factual presentation, and the credibility of management's statements will largely be a function of their personal credibility with fund managers. That partly explains why management credibility is as high on a fund manager's list of decision-making criteria as disclosure. It's all on trust because so relatively little is measured and disclosed. I will have much to say about this in Chapter 11.

Of course, what creates long-term value in most businesses is not always easily measured. How do you measure customer satisfaction, the quality of the research process or staff morale? But, usually, if there is a will there is a way of finding robust measures – retention rates of existing customers and the acquisition rate of new customers, retention rates of core staff, the robustness of the brand franchise (via measures such as share of voice or recall rates), scrap rates, core customer profitability, employee productivity, etc.

Operating indicators tend to be used by line management at divisional level more than by corporate management. They may not even be seen by corporate. Each core division is likely to have two to three lead operating indicators. Often, the metrics will vary by division. What is a lead indicator for the cosmetics division will be irrelevant to the detergents division. It is likely that a subset of lead indicators will be relevant across multiple divisions or across the majority of the company's revenue base. These will probably not have been disclosed to investors other than anecdotally, but they may prove to be more reliable guides to long-term cashflow performance than historical financials alone.

What about the analysts in this mix? Surely, they go to great pains to analyse sector trends, to explore operating metrics and to interrogate financials? First, all analysts are fundamentally reliant on what information the company will give them and also on getting their interpretation of the numbers. Companies are careful to vet analysts' projections for clear factual error before they go out. A company keen on minimising disclosure can usually get its own way and this causes much complaint amongst the best sell-side analysts. Second, analysts' forecasts are primarily concerned with earnings-related sensitivities and reliability of earnings a year out. Indicators of longer term performance are typically a secondary concern and when discussed are usually more upbeat, as there is less accountability and greater margin for error. As a result, I would suggest that many large-cap fund managers do not pay them that much attention. This is an issue to be addressed by management.

How valuable is the value story as a value lever?

One of the sources of misvaluation we discussed in Chapter 2 is that markets estimate value based on extrapolations into the future from current numbers. If a current number falls away by 50% the market tends to take that as the benchmark for future earnings, so that a new base earnings number is set for valuation purposes. The use of PE multiples creates the same effect. Fluctuations in current base numbers produce large variances in valuation. Just because a company misses its current forecast, this does not mean it will not restore profitability going forward. But, that is how the markets often read it. A missed number is met with a disproportionate fall in value. The attention of management, analysts and investors is therefore firmly on annual numbers.

The challenge we discussed in Chapter 8 was how to strike a better balance between the focus on the annual forecast and what I call the "value story". Would disclosure of more facts and indicators of drivers of the value story be a method of balancing out short-term volatility and keeping the company more reliably in the fair value corridor? Our research suggests that different types of institutional fund managers will place different weight on forecasts v. the value story. In general, there was some evidence to suggest that engaged value-determining investors would potentially be more prepared to pay attention to the value story. This appears to raise the opportunity for deepening disclosure in selective areas as a value lever. But, as always, the decision about what to disclose is not straightforward. For example, an active insurance fund manager may place a particular focus on management quality, and product life cycle, both of which are longer term value story areas. A hedge fund manager, by contrast, may have no interest in the value story and be focused on 1-year margin performance against forecast. If, as in this case, both fund managers are value-determining investors, then management have some tough decisions to make regarding their disclosure priorities.

One major challenge with the value story is that, to be robust, it requires the disclosure of a range of competitive and operating measures. This presents the challenge of identifying what measures are most relevant, how they might be reliably measured and ideally compared across the sector. It also raises the issue of how to quantify whether the risks of disclosing them, in terms of unreliability of data, of giving a false picture and also of setting the company up for disappointment, outweigh the potential benefits to investors. This means that, in seeking to place emphasis on the value story, the disclosure issue has to be thoroughly analysed. What information is critical to those investors that matter and where will deeper disclosure really drive value? Where is deeper disclosure achievable with reliability? Few companies go through an analytical process to identify where their disclosure priorities should lie. That is where I will spend the rest of this chapter.

Before going further down this path, I should point out that what was also clear from our research was that not all companies could even attempt to shift focus from the

Table 9.1 A basic expectation management framework

	Focus	Objective	Responsible
Forecast (half- and full-year)	• Revenue growth • Margins • EPS growth	Exceed peer and sector mean Exceed market expectations	CEO Finance group IR
Value story (2 years +)	• Sources of revenue growth • Basis of margin enhancement • Corporate strategy	Substantiate fair valuation	CEO Finance group Strategy group IR Divisional management

annual forecast to the value story. Management in effect have to win the right to take a longer term view and for it to be taken seriously. This means that they need to have proven they can deliver on annual forecasts with predictability (Table 9.1). Therefore, it would appear that the value story may be better suited to keeping a good performing company in the fair value corridor than helping a fallen company return to it. In order to get back in the fair value corridor the markets need

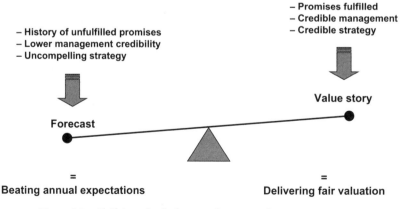

Figure 9.3 Shifting the balance of expectation management.

to gain confidence in annual delivery. Fair value is not a quick fix.

Towards the selectively open kimono

There have been a number of research attempts to support the proposition that deepened disclosure can in general boost returns to shareholders. However, none of the evidence is convincing and many of the strongest advocates are no longer so evangelical about it as there has been little uptake by companies. Rephrasing the research to ask the question whether deepened disclosure might help a company achieve fair value appears much more fruitful. But with some caveats. The disclosure must above all be relevant to the investors that matter and the risk of disclosure as well as potential rewards must be fully understood. On the basis of our research and building on existing methodologies, we have structured a simple approach to helping companies determine whether selectively deepening disclosure can be a lever to keeping them in the fair value corridor.[1]

The process starts with hypothesis generation by the company and a set of simple self-interrogations. Where is our disclosure comparatively thin compared with immediate peers? From what we know of our institutional investors, do we believe there are potential hot buttons that would impact value-determining investors? Are there particular disclosure items that we believe might help us move value-

---

[1] See Eccles et al., PricewaterhouseCoopers (2001).

Table 9.2 Step 1 – Identifying major disclosure gaps.

Category	Industry/ competitive	Strategic	Financial performance	Operational data
Disclosure gap	• Market growth • Market share • Brand awareness • Regulatory pressures • Margin trends	• Strategic direction • Acquisition objectives • Divestiture targets • "Quality of management"	• Free cashflow • Performance by business segment • WACC • CAPEX • Revenue from new products	• Productivity • Quality control • Staff turnover • Client/ customer churn

determining investors from focusing on forecasts to the value story? Provisionally at least, do we believe these are data we can reliably measure and which will provide real insight into our future value creation? Our research would suggest that such hot buttons and areas of opportunity will fall into four broad categories (Table 9.2 illustrates what an initial screen of opportunity areas might look like):

• Industry/competitive data.

• Strategic information.

• Operational data.

• Financial metrics.

Insights into where potential disclosure gaps may lie can come from a number of sources. Management will have some intuition about the areas of information that have historically driven major shareprice movements, through from client loss to restatements of assets or reserves. Divisional management will also have a better feel for operational measures which may be oriented towards fleshing out the value story. Ideally, having completed the investor screening analysis in Chapter 6, the company could extend the same model to correlate the unique movements in shareprice against disclosure events – from earnings, to strategy and even to management change. In the absence of existing management intuition, such analysis may give some insight into where deepened disclosure is likely to create advantage.

Another good source of clues is competitors disclosing more deeply than we are and researching what the apparent impact has been on shareprice. Again, areas of differentiation could fall into any of the four major disclosure areas. A third source of insight into disclosure gaps is analysis of comparative disclosure by analogous quoted sectors. For example, if your business is in the automotive component sector, do similarly sized businesses in consumer goods manufacture disclose more deeply in a range of areas? Can they offer clues as to where deepened disclosure holds potential competitive advantage, particularly as regards the value story?

The result of such data gathering and introspection should be a fairly long list of hypotheses regarding significant disclosure gaps. The trick is knowing where elimination of gaps will help deliver fair value, reducing the gulf between management's estimate of enterprise value and that of value-determining investors. A simple method of prioritising disclosure gaps is to interrogate the value attached to them

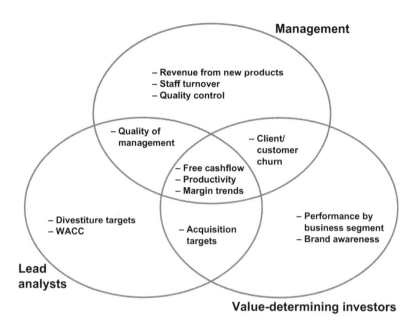

Figure 9.4 Identifying where disclosure gaps matter.

by the three core constituencies – value-determining investors, lead sell-side analysts and management themselves.

Having identified those fund managers that qualify as value-determining investors, the first step into deepening the dialogue with them can be asking them to prioritise and add to the list of initial disclosure gaps identified by management. They may even contribute their own. Either way, this will offer direct insight into their decision-making criteria.

Management cannot, however, fall into the trap of simply giving fund managers what they say they want. Value-determining investors will also almost certainly change to some extent over a 6-month period and therefore the company has to consider disclosure issues that may be relevant to a broader constituency of such active fund managers. Many will not have the same level of insight about value creation in the particular business as management. Management may have insights into future value generation and indicators of value generation which are ahead of that of their primary fund managers. The real challenge could well be "educating" these funds through the disclosure process.

Nor can the company ignore the lead sell-side analyst community, as they are influencers of fund manager opinion. Therefore, their insights into disclosure gaps also need to be taken into account, particularly as regards the use of metrics to back up the value story. The resulting screening process should help management identify clear priority areas for deeper disclosure which will in all likelihood be a subset of their initial list. Given the turnover in value-determining investors, changes in disclosure by competitors and ever-shifting market sentiment, such disclosure screening should be an annual process. This will in effect lead to ever-greater levels of disclosure but of a highly targeted nature.

None of this comes without its risks. The more that is measured the more there is to manage in the public gaze and less room for "gaming". The challenge for management will be that a number of the priority disclosure gaps will present an unacceptable level of risk. A value-determining fund manager may place a high value on understanding client churn rates but if these are misleading because of a strategy of migrating to a smaller number of global customers, then it may tell the wrong message. Managing the disclosure transition requires careful judgement and is often most

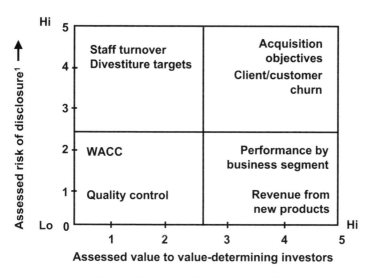

Figure 9.5 Assessing the cost/benefits of deepened disclosure on core items.
[1] Competitive data risk/exposure of underperformance risk/unreliable data risk.

difficult in situations of overvaluation where the latent fear is serious correction.

One answer is for management to perform a basic version of risk–reward analysis (Figure 9.5). This will help them think through where disclosure gaps represent a viable trade-off. Calibrating risk is not straightforward, and will involve a weighting of risk from poor data quality, the market risk that might arise from disclosure to competitors, and risk that such data might be subject to misinterpretation by shareholders. The reward side of the equation is, of course, no easier to gauge. However, the initial screening of disclosure gaps with the core constituencies will have lent some insight into where real rewards may lie.

Our research would suggest that the primary opportunity set lies in disclosure related to the value story, where the risks of increased disclosure may be more palatable to management and more manageable, and where competitive advantage with fund managers v. competitors may be the highest. But, the challenge of picking the right disclosure items, establishing robust metrics and ensuring they provide insight into value creation, is all the greater in this area. The best measures tend to be those that are relevant internally to divisional management and are therefore linked to internal measures of performance. They may even have been tried and tested in the context of a balanced scorecard.

To tell or not to tell ...

Ultimately, logic and empirical research would point to the conclusion that a company with deeper disclosure will ultimately be more accurately valued than a company with lower disclosure. Management credibility will be higher and the number of sources of "surprise" potentially reduced. In other words, the market price will more closely approximate to fair value. But, knowing where disclosure should be deepened and, perhaps more importantly, when it should be deepened, is a process that demands careful thought and analysis.

Our research would suggest that disclosure can be an effective general value lever (with different disclosure items constituting value levers in their own right) both for a company that is seeking to manage its position within the fair value corridor and for the company that is seeking to return to it. Returning to the fair value corridor from a position of undervaluation relies on management re-establishing trust with fund managers, as we will discuss in detail in Chapter 11. Deepening disclosure and demonstrating improvement on a range of performance metrics is one effective way of building confidence, provided the organisation can subsequently deliver. Of course, deciding where the company can tell investors more is only one part of the equation. The other key part is how you tell them. That is where we go next.

10

Deciding how to tell investors

The art of managing communications channels

Y OU MIGHT THINK THAT WITH THE AVERAGE FTSE
company having 40 or more institutional investors,
the communications process would not be complicated. How wrong you would be. The investor relations
role is an intensely demanding one. It spans responsibility
for the annual report, the website, half- and full-year results
announcements, the AGM and perhaps three of four major
analysts' gatherings a year, an ongoing process of public
relations and press management, and response to around
30–40 daily calls or emails from smaller investors.

The most demanding aspect of the job is probably organising
meetings between the executive team and fund managers. We
have discussed how many companies segment their investors
on two dimensions – size of their holding and geographical
location. On this basis the Investor Relations (IR) director
usually draws up a procession of annual meetings. Investor
groups holding above 1% of the shares in issue are on average

allotted two meetings per year, and groups with less than this one meeting per year. Funds with particularly large holdings of, say, above 3% will typically be the subject of a number of interactions, both face to face and on the phone. Overseas investors, in other words European and US investors, are typically dealt with in a single week-long "road show" each. This means that, in total, investor meetings typically number around 70 or so for the average firm in a normal year.

Who researches the contents, orchestrates the messages and manages delivery for these meetings? As we have discussed, many large companies conduct relatively little analysis of their shareholders. Nor do they typically put huge effort into researching and honing the messages they communicate in these meetings, beyond a consensus on core forecast numbers. Moreover, the IR director is rarely the presenter. The role of the IR director in the process is often largely logistical – fixing the mind-bending complexity of room bookings, attendee lists and materials preparation. The core contents of the presentation are usually generated by the finance group, perhaps with input from the strategy group, and the same presentation is used for an entire year unless events change dramatically. Much of the flavour and customisation is down to the CEO's personal presentation technique.

Compare this for a moment with the typical marketing process for a large company. When a company communicates with a particular customer group, usually its interactions are highly planned and orchestrated. A budget will be drawn up by the marketing director, brand messages researched and established, communications channels chosen. Then weightings will be applied to particular channels, whether advertising, direct marketing, promotions or a range of other options, and appropriate rates negotiated with the media owners. Retrospectively, the efficiency of the communications spend in terms of both customer impact and financial returns is likely to be researched. In other words, there is a clear managerial discipline and a level of "science" to the process. The focus is on consistency of message, and coherence of the media chosen. One person is ultimately accountable and results are the subject of research.

The IR process, itself a communication event with perhaps the most important customer group of all, looks very different. The process of communications with investors has certain predictable elements to it – the AGM, the annual report, analysts' presentations. But, it also has lots of *ad hoc*, largely unorchestrated elements to it – impromptu meetings with individual fund managers, press releases, daily responses to emails and phone calls, press interviews. If you draw up even the roughest chart laying out the various strands, then it becomes clear what a complex tapestry of communications it actually is, and precisely how much is conducted on the hoof rather than being part of a planned campaign (Figure 10.1). There are a large range of types of communications that can roughly be divided into direct, one-to-one communications and mass communications. There are also a fairly wide range of people from the corporate centre involved, from the executive team, to the IR director to the director of strategy. Consistency and accountability are far less clear than with the marketing process.

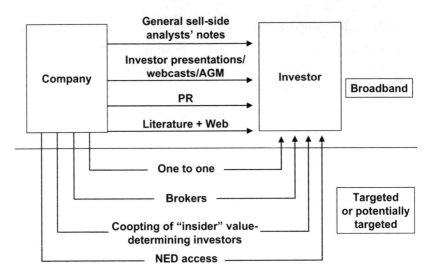

Figure 10.1   A typical investor communications mix.
NED = Non Executive Director.

For the highly organised marketing director this would look like a nightmare. Where is the customer understanding? Where is the decision on brand values and messages? Where is the accountability for the mediums chosen? Who is actually doing what? Where is the unifying strategy? Often, the answer is there doesn't appear to be one. Whilst marketing has evolved a useful set of methodologies for helping professionals make decisions about communications choices, IR appears to be singularly devoid of any such models. Isn't it time to let the marketing people take over this muddle and sort it out?

On the other side of the equation, the question to ask is should the investor communications process actually look like a marketing event at all, as a number of commentators have suggested? Is its complexity and unpredictability part of the nature of dealing with this singular constituency? Would thinking along the classic marketing lines of customer segmentation, brand message and medium really be workable? The answer is not clear-cut. Since IR concerns itself with the fate of the company, one would assume a great deal of time and thought would be invested in researching the likely response of its core shareholders to certain events and what influence different types of communication might have on its shareholder base. You might also assume that the company would have analysed the efficacy of different mediums of communication and therefore weighted its activity formally. In fact, our research would suggest that the IR process is often an intensely tactical one, responding to events rather than following a proactive strategy.

Our research would also suggest that it is a highly personalised process, based on intuition and feel rather than analysis. The face of the process is vested with the CEO and CFO. Much of investor insight is generated from their "feel" for the fund managers, and much of the corporate communications strategy is a function of what they choose to say at certain times and with certain people. We have already talked about the personalisation of the investor interface and the perils it holds. This personalisation is reinforced by the roadshow dimension of the IR process. In effect, there is little professionalised communications framework. The IR director will sometimes have relatively little credibility with major fund managers. They will want to hear it from the CEO.

As a by-product of this personalisation of the communications process, there tends to be little measurement of the effectiveness of different communications events. Are certain formats better than others? Does the general investor presentation used for analysts also work effectively in one-to-one meetings with key fund managers? Is there a correlation between the number of meetings with fund managers and the length of their average hold? What would be the optimal split between time and resources spent on one-to-one communications events with fund managers v. mass marketing to larger audiences? The annual report now costs the average FTSE 100 company something approaching £1m to design, print and distribute. But, it is impossible to find any convincing research as to the impact on institutional fund managers. The same is fast becoming true of corporate websites which are mostly digitised versions of the hard copy.

In the general marketing sphere, there has been a remorseless shift of spend away from mass communications towards more targeted and responsive communications events that are broadly grouped under the epithet "direct marketing". In reality, direct marketing covers a large range of different communications tools, from database-driven CRM through to promotional events. The same logic would appear relevant to communications with investors. Surely, it would make more sense to pour resource into one-on-one dialogues with value-determining investors than to spray money at as blunt an instrument as the annual report or an ever more lavish website? Given we are talking about a small number of individuals who matter, wouldn't it also make sense to customise the messages we give them?

The back-drop to this scene is the increasing amount of regulatory pressure on disclosure. It is simply not viable to

Figure 10.2   Measuring the efficiency of the communications process.

abandon general analysts' meetings, to slim down the annual report, to abandon the website. If a company were to do so it would quickly run the risk of contravening stock exchange regulations. To some degree, the value-determining investor has, by dint of law, to be treated the same as the retail punter. The information flow has to be equally available to them both. The reality is that the line is blurred, and companies clearly invest more of their time behind their core investors. But, nevertheless, the constraint is there.

So, assuming that we have identified our value-determining investors and got a good grasp of their patterns of behaviour, how can the communications process be made more effective in altering perceptions and conditioning behaviours, particularly amongst those fund managers that really matter? That's where we go next.

Towards an investor communications strategy

The first question in any communications process is who are we trying to communicate with? Much of this book has been about identifying those investors that matter and understanding their behaviour. For the company that chooses to pursue a fair value strategy, the communications process should be made all the simpler because it will be clear where to invest energy. It will also be clearer what type of messages will be more impactful with them. This will mean a decisive shift towards targeted communications rather than mass communications.

In this scenario, websites and annual reports are likely to become hygiene factors and not sources of competitive advantage. There is likely to be more mileage in targeted mediums than mass mediums. Reliance solely on general sell-side analysts' channels may not be adequate. Customisation of the message and the medium all has to delivered within the context of respecting general disclosure rules. But, it may be conceivable that it would be better to shift both content and format to reflect issues that will influence active managers rather than the "average" investor – mass communications but with highly particular relevance.

Part of this focusing exercise will be gaining an understanding of how such active fund managers get their information and what channels get their attention. This will vary case by case, but there will always be a reasonably predictable level of hierarchy. It is likely that the fund manager will most highly value one-to-one meetings and direct executive access. Given finite management time, decisive decisions have to be made to prioritise certain investors over others. Rather than relying on size and geography as the determinants of this roll-call, the priority will be value-determining investors, with the balance of time for the rest.

Beyond direct interaction, it is likely that value-determining investors will be influenced by certain analysts. Again, understanding precisely which they are and what opinions they hold will be vital. It is also likely that certain brokers will have an influence on their trading activity. This will call for detective work to identify where the key relationships lie and to strategise how such advisers could themselves be influenced. Beyond these two channels it will probably be far less clear where sources of influence lie. It might be with certain journals or commentators, with something as simple as the half-yearly results presentation or as complex as the rumour mill. A major input of the IR group should be a review of likely influencers on value-determining investors.

One possible conclusion of such research may be a blank – it does not seem that any of these channels hold particular opportunities to influence our key constituency of fund managers. Sure, they get the analysts' notes, they do take meetings with management, but their actions do not appear to emerge as a result of that interface. This is a common situation and leads to the sort of frustration you often hear expressed by management – *"He nodded in the meeting, he seemed to have read the analyst note and then he went and sold. What do you have to do?"*

The role of indirect signalling

Our research suggests that the reason these situations arise is that active fund managers are often not particularly swayed by what management tell them. They regard such meetings and conversations as a marketing effort by management and therefore discount them. They also acknowledge that some sell-side analysts, however capable, often see the future through rose-tinted spectacles. Instead, what influences their perceptions are what could be called indirect signals of value – things that happen or are said which give pointers towards likely future performance. Our research suggests that such indirect signals may often be more powerful than direct communications.

Sometimes, management will have given relatively little thought to the role of indirect signalling devices and their possible impact. However, at one point or another they are likely to have used a number of them. Such indirect signals include such actions as shifts in buy-back or dividend policy. They include changes to executive structure and compensation, such as the appointment of non-executive directors or the institution of a stock option plan. They include adjustments to an existing strategy, such as the decision to acquire or divest. Broadly speaking, such indirect signalling devices can be clustered into three areas:

- Signals that affect capital structure.

- Signals that affect management structure and incentives.

- Signals that affect strategy.

A shift from a policy of applying free cashflow to acquisitions to applying it to a share buy-back programme might send a clear signal that management view the shares as undervalued. The reverse may send the signal that management regards the shareprice as high and they feel it would be prudent to use that currency to acquire new profit streams. This may be a more palatable approach to easing down the shareprice than a bare statement that growth expectations are beyond what the company can deliver. Equally, the announcement of a decision by the management team to instate a new remuneration scheme that pays out in shares based on steep earnings growth targets might send a signal about what management believe is possible. Alternatively, the decision to replace a non-executive from a deal-oriented background with another that has been closely associated with cost-cutting might help slow down a run-away shareprice. The number of permutations are very large indeed.

Within the three broad areas of indirect signalling, there are potentially a large number of levers available to management. Indeed, anyone reading this with responsibility for the IR function will be able to think of many I have not. Two major issues are raised by attempting to use these indirect signalling devices. First, based on our observations, it is likely that it will be more impactful if more than one signalling device is used together. For example, use of share buy-backs will carry more weight if it is combined with director share purchases and an aggressive compensation plan as a signal of undervaluation. Conversely, the dropping of share buy-backs, combined with a change of non-executives, and the execution of a really large acquisition, may begin to send the signal that the shares are at fair value.

Second, coordination of a number of signalling devices raises the issue of who does the coordinating? It is likely that different levers will fall under the control of different departments and different individuals. This means that someone, and presumably the IR director, will need to articulate a compelling case for combining actions with the objective of altering perceptions by value-determining investors. This calls for strategy, for research, for proactivity – not qualities our research suggested currently always underpins the average IR function.

Back to basics . . .

The use of indirect signalling devices does not mean that management should in some way abandon the communications process. Indeed, it would appear that there are often opportunities to improve on the basics. First, all communications can benefit from honing and refining the message. The average active large-cap fund manager has very little capacity to absorb inputs on a particular company. Often, they will have what amounts to a crib sheet of five or six key points. It is essential that, having worked out what is driving their behaviour, management simplify the message as far as possible, distilling it down to a handful of key points or, in marketing parlance, core messages.

Companies do not always think that hard about how they look to outsiders. They don't see the inconsistencies, they don't see the messy edges – the businesses that don't quite fit, the geographical coverage that doesn't quite make sense. Companies are just like people. If someone is hard to understand, if we can't place them, we usually don't bother. Many investors want to feel they can quickly get their hands around the company, they want simplicity, and they want to be able to pigeon-hole.

There would also appear to be opportunities in many instances to increase the weight given to the value story by picking appropriately compelling measures. Too often in the communications process the value story is simply an addendum to the annual forecast. This can be an opportunity missed. How can the company work with lead analysts to focus attention on forward-looking market, strategic and operating measures that support the fair value objectives of the company? The willingness of fund managers to absorb the value story will be very contingent on management credibility, something we will explore in Chapter 11. It may also be conditioned by the strength of the corporate brand, again something we will explore in Chapter 11.

Our research would also suggest that often insufficient thought is given to the communications mix. Should as much time and resource be poured into the annual report and website? Would time be better invested working with lead sell-side analysts to hone their models and bring them closer to the internal valuation process? Could the number of investor meetings be reduced in favour of greater interaction with value-determining investors? Could the PR firm supporting the company better target messages at active fund managers?

Finally, all of this supposes a willingness to commit resource to analysing the institutional investor base in the first place. Without an understanding of individual fund managers, communications targeting is impossible. To ensure that its chosen communications channels are delivering, management also have to invest energy in gauging their effectiveness with fund managers (a simplified version of such a piece of analysis in illustrated in Figure 10.2). In short, whilst investor communications cannot be thought of as a classic marketing process, it can potentially learn from some of the basic tools of the marketing trade such as the discipline of focus and accountability.

11

The role of management quality

Setting the fair value context

C OUNTLESS ACADEMIC STUDIES HAVE ATTEMPTED TO determine what influences fund managers' decisions to buy shares. These studies vary in terms of sophistication and breadth, but the top of the list of factors is always the same (perhaps disappointingly so for erstwhile researchers) – "quality of management". If you believed the surveys, then the holy grail would be clear – be a good manager and the investors will surely follow (Figure 11.1).

There are usually a couple of peculiarities to these surveys. By "management", surveys tend to mean primarily two people – the CEO and CFO – although this can extend to the MD, chairman and non-executive directors (NEDs). It is an odd feature of large companies, most of which will have been around for years and seen many CEOs come and go, that the process of creating share value is perceived to be so dependent on one or two individuals. This gives rise to many obvious questions. If the average tenure of a CEO is

Figure 11.1 What factors most influence how fund managers select a particular stock (% of respondents citing critical factor)?
Source: Adapted from IRS data (2002).

3 years, how can they alone be attributed with building long-term value? What about the countless other managers at the coalface? Surely they count?

The second peculiarity is understanding precisely how "quality" is measured in this context? Most surveys alight on one measure of quality above all others – track record (Figure 11.2). In other words, what matters is that management have delivered a similar game for shareholders in the past and are therefore a safe pair of hands. But, is track record a reliable predictor of future performance? If so, how should an individual's track record be measured? There is, after all, no independent service that gauges what an individual has directly contributed in their previous roles – there is no equivalent of Standard and Poor's or Moody's for management. The more you press on this issue of "quality of management", the more fungible it becomes.

Also, does this logic hold true in practice? If it did you would expect that, when an under-rated company replaces its CEO with a new CEO with an appropriate track record, that there would be an immediate and sustained recovery in value. In fact, our research would suggest that the up-tick of the positive news tends to be a short-lived effect. On average, within 2 months the shareprice will have settled back to within 5% of where it was before the appointment. This would suggest

Figure 11.2 How do fund managers identify "good management" (% of respondents citing critical factor)?
Source: Adapted from IRS data (2002).

that, whilst investors focus their attentions on the individual, they are sanguine enough to realise there is far more to it. Just because the new guy is in, they still have to create real value to sustain a higher valuation. It also suggests that, in many large-cap fund managers' minds, "management quality" encompasses a view of the entire management and board as a whole and its ability to deliver reliable results. It does not rest just with the CEO.

The emphasis on the individual may in large part be a product of corporate culture rather than an invention of the investor community. CEOs often tend to personalise the investor management process and err in the direction of conflating their personal equity with that of the company. In fact, our research would imply that a charismatic CEO is likely to introduce more volatility into a stock than would be experienced by a company where management is institutionalised rather than individualised. Many companies that go through valuation surges and eventually suffer corrections tend to be ruled by a highly personalised management style. The CEO will be a star – a magician attributed with miraculous powers of strategy and insight by the likes of Forbes and CNN. In essence, they will tend to be good self-promoters – expert at harnessing the press, keen on maintaining a high profile and inclined towards a strategy of maximising shareprice.

This is probably putting too negative a spin on the power of the individual. To turn a small company into a large one you have to win the confidence of investors. You have to be able to attract talent that otherwise would gravitate to more established businesses. You have to be able to win over customers who would more naturally turn to incumbent providers. In this entrepreneurial battle, a magnetic personality is often the glue that holds the show together. The defining characteristic of the company is its boss.

But, within a large, mature, established business, life is very different. Product cycles will be long. Management structures will be well-established. Customer relationships will be engrained. In short, it should have evolved from being a personal business to being more akin to an institution. The appearance of the entrepreneur in this environment can be highly disruptive. An overwhelming impulse to stamp a personal mark will initiate change in pursuit of higher growth. The company may also be likely to become more susceptible to the logic of M&A as a solution to everything. Strategy is likely to be revised completely. The company is likely to turn from a value stock into a growth stock. The result tends to be entry to the shareprice circus – a steep re-rating followed in all probability by a sharp correction.

Given that institutional fund managers appear to place such store in "quality of management", can this cycle be avoided? Part of the issue clearly lies in the selection of the CEO and FD and the circumstances of their appointment. Have they been brought in from outside to make a clean sweep or have they been promoted from inside? But, much of the issue also lies in how the company manages the "management quality"

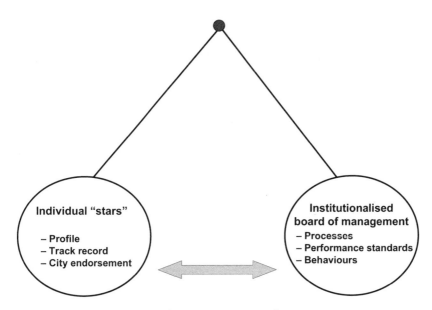

Figure 11.3 Good governance v. good management.

card. Is there a conscious objective of avoiding personalised identification with an individual to overall regard for the management of the business, in other words the board as a whole? Our research would suggest that companies that incline towards a fair value strategy tend to de-emphasize the role of the CEO and emphasize the quality of the board, management processes and what could broadly be called "governance". On the pendulum illustrated in Figure 11.3, the company is likely to be firmly weighted to the right.

This objective is not some democratic, academic pipe-dream. It is consistent with what many surveys have noted about how fund managers and analysts gauge the quality of a company and the quality of its management. High up on the fund manager's agenda are always references to "trustworthiness", "openness" and "quality of control". In essence, what this boils down to is the question of whether the company employs a system of checks and balances to ensure investor interests are protected? It is this that constitutes good management in a broad sense or what is commonly referred to as "good governance".

Good governance as good investor strategy?

Ever since the meltdown of companies such as Enron and WorldCom, "governance" has been a term bandied around in every management journal going. It is almost as ubiquitous and as vacuous as the term "strategy". Everyone wants to claim they have a good governance process, the same as they are keen to persuade everyone they have a strategy. But, what does it mean to be well-governed? "Good governance" is almost as indefinable a concept as good management. How do you measure it? How do you tell good governance from bad until something goes wrong? Is a well-managed company synonymous with a well-governed company? Do investors really reward good governance?

There is reasonable evidence to support the notion that well-governed companies are indeed valued more highly by investors (Figure 11.4). It is also logical that a well-governed company, like the company that tends towards deeper disclosure, will be more fairly valued. Therefore, it makes sense that a company pursuing a fair value strategy would also have thought hard about its approach to governance,

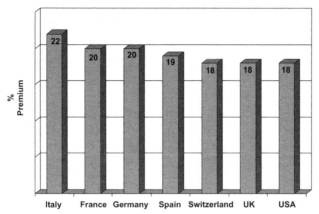

Figure 11.4 Average premium that investors are willing to pay for a well-governed company, by country (%).
Source: Adapted from McKinsey Investor Opinion Survey, 1999–2000.

and how it might enable investors to distinguish it on this basis from other competitors.

Whilst many companies view governance as a hygiene factor, our research suggested that few think of it as a source of competitive advantage. This is not exactly surprising. Most companies feel they operate in a highly regulated environment. There are accountancy standards, stock exchange rules, FSA regulations, a range of best practice standards that have emerged from the Cadbury Code, the Combined Code, the Myners Report, the Higgs Report and the various other reports into governance issues over the years. There is legislation surrounding redundancy and health and safety. There are the growing legal implications of director responsibility. To the over-stretched executive, the list can appear endless and growing.

However, it can be equally argued that most UK and US companies operate in what amounts to a highly deregulated environment. There is great leeway in interpretation of even the most basic accountancy rules. There is great leeway when it comes to boardroom practice. The various codes tend to be suggestions of best practice and not company law. There is also typically an imperfect process of monitoring and policing best practices. The regulatory framework is largely a matter of self-policing and honesty. What really matters in a deregulated environment is the quality of self-regulation. That is why honesty and openness make it to the top of the fund manager list of what is perceived to constitute good management (Figure 11.4).

At the core of the self-regulation process is the non-executive function – the "independent" presence representing the interests of shareholders. Best practice, most fully articulated in the Combined Code and updated by the Higgs Report, suggests that non-execs should comprise at least three out of a board of six, so around a half of the voting board. This is about where most large quoted companies fall. More importantly, it is also suggested that the core committees – Remuneration, Nomination and Audit – should be controlled by the non-executive group and that the chairman should be a non-executive, supported by a senior non-executive with influence sufficient to check the power of the CEO. It is the fiduciary requirement of this group to advance shareholder interests at all times. But, is that what happens in practice?

Typically, non-execs are seasoned figures from industry who have at one point or another held a senior executive post themselves. Their average age is around 54, and the average non-exec holds slightly over two such positions, paying a salary of around £30,000 per post. Traditionally, the role has been something of a dying elephant's graveyard. The great and the good saw out their last years in due dignity, supplementing their pensions. Things have moved on. It is now clear to all that non-execs share the same fiduciary duties as their executive brethren and therefore cannot afford to fall asleep at the wheel, particularly when it comes to thorny issues, such as compensation.

Interestingly, between 1980 and 2001 the average age of the FTSE 100 non-exec fell from 57 years to 54. Their number also increased from around 350 to more than 400. It appears that their role is being taken more seriously and they are taking their role more seriously. In the past, the non-exec group would typically change with the CEO or chairman – loyalties would be very clear. But, now the average non-exec actually has a longer tenure than the CEO – averaging slightly over 4 years v. the CEO's 3 years. As a result, there is the potential to de-couple personal loyalties and non-exec management, something which has traditionally been hard to achieve.

However, potential flaws still exist in the self-regulatory role of most non-executive board structures. First, there is the very practical issue of acting as interventionists from a position of part-time employment. The typical non-exec attends six board meetings a year. They typically receive a board pack 4 days before the meeting, detailing financial performance and issues to be aired. Given the complexity of most companies, there is little hope of them launching any substantive inquiry into the business. This is particularly so as non-execs tend not to have grown up in the same industry as the company on whose board they sit. They may also be tacitly discouraged from sticking the boot into tough issues because any minuted observations about performance have to be made available to the auditors who will demand disclosure. The result is that non-exec boards tend not to have real "teeth".

The incentive for most non-execs to take an interventionist stance is also undermined by the compensation arrangements surrounding their appointment. The average non-exec fee is £30,000. The average board meeting is 5 hours long. Six of those a year, plus some extras, is around 50 hours a year which works out at £600 per hour. That may not sound unattractive, but if this is adjusted for the risk taken by the non-exec, which is exactly the same risk run by the CEO on £1.5m a year, then it is not so good. Who would risk personal liability for £30,000 a year? Typically not successful current executives of other businesses. The result is self-selection. Most non-execs in large PLCs run small portfolios of such positions generating income of perhaps £100,000 in total.

Combine this basis of motivation with the frequently eccentric selection process for non-execs and there is the beginning of a flaw. In the past almost all non-execs were appointed overtly from the network of the CEO or chairman. This has now become more subtle, and many companies will appoint a search firm to generate a short list which is vetted. The proposed non-exec is ultimately approved through interview with the CEO or chairman. There may be a small amount of vetting with a couple of institutional fund managers but it will probably not be substantive unless the appointment is as a result of a major management reshuffle.

Probably the single most important contribution of non-execs is their participation on the Audit Committee, the Remuneration Committee and to a lesser extent, the Nomination Committee. Best practice suggests that all three committees should be dominated by, if not exclusively manned by non-execs. This, in principle, should give non-execs very considerable power over management, but it also raises some thorny issues. Senior executive compensation is probably the most inflammatory issue the board habitually faces. It is also the most visible to institutional shareholders. Then there is Audit which is perhaps the most complex and technical area the company faces in terms of its interface with external constituencies.

A potential flaw is, once again, a very practical one. Both tasks are supposed to be overseen and recommendations made to the board by a group of individuals contracted to devote 12 working days a year to the company. In the case of senior executive compensation, they are presented with a complex proposal prepared by a dedicated professional, typically the director of HR. The same is true of audit and financial reports which will be produced by the CFO. They will typically receive a briefing note and a list of sign-offs by the auditors. By the time they are consulted on both, they tend to be *fait accomplis*. The only real option NEDs have if they disagree is to contest the proposal which is an intensely confrontational thing to do and as a result rarely done. Non-execs who are interventionist often continually teeter on the edge of resignation, and this is too exhausting a position to maintain for long.

The role of the non-exec is often viewed by executive management in the same way as disclosure – it is a necessary inconvenience to be kept under wraps. Of course, institutional fund managers, brokers and analysts are entirely cognoscent of this reality. For this reason they rarely, if ever, meet with the non-execs or solicit their opinion. Non-execs rarely have direct exposure to investors and their views are seldom reflected in analysts' notes or in the annual report. The markets also pay less interest in their share-dealings than with executive management. All eyes are on the executive team and specifically the CEO. The common attitude to the non-exec board is born of the cult of the individual that underpins the strategy of shareprice maximisation.

Governance as a value lever

Based on our research, it would appear viable to believe that good governance can contribute to a fair value strategy. Governance is high on the agenda of fund managers and trustees of pension funds. It has also permeated the analyst community. Good governance offers the ability to detract from the focus solely on the CEO as star which characterises shareprice maximisation strategies. A well-governed company would in principle appear to be one in which long-term investment is appropriate, mitigating churn of the register and associated volatility.

But, in practice, who is to say what a well-governed company looks like? Whilst the Cadbury and Combined Codes, supplemented with the various subsequent reports from Myners to Higgs, suggest the elements that would be desirable, there is only a partial benchmark of best practice that is expected by fund managers and analysts. This is of course both a problem and an opportunity. The problem is that a company might invest lots of energy in a governance process, only to see its efforts fall on disinterested fund managers' ears. The opportunity is that, for those companies who can set the standards and set the basis of measurement, there is a unique advantage to be gained, particularly if such a framework is used to communicate quality of management to investors as part of a fair value process.

As part of the research process, we reviewed the various recommendations that have been made to improve governance and distilled them into four groups of core principles (Table 11.1):

- That the directorship is capable of delivering reliably.

- That it is self-reflective and objective in its judgements.

- That it is held accountable for results.

- And that it responds to the inputs and goals of investors.

It is likely that a well-governed company will achieve some sort of equilibrium between the four attributes. An accountable board with balanced objectives is likely to under-perform if it is not responsive to investor opinion and inflexible. A highly responsive board, but one which lacks the objectivity to interrogate its objectives, is unlikely to be a high performer. Table 11.1 illustrates the simple sort of criteria a company can use to gauge its performance on these attributes. A clear, and ideally measured, assessment of performance against these parameters would allow clear communication

Table 11.1 Assessing the quality of governance

Capable	• Company track record against expectations available to investors • Individual directors' career track records disclosed to investors • Historical analyst ratings pattern • Number of incidents of disclosed fraud
Objective	• 50% of directors are NEDs • 50% of Nomination Committees are occupied by NEDs • Separation of CEO/chairman role • Presence of senior NED • NED appointments approved by major institutional investors
Accountable	• 75% of Remuneration Committees are occupied by NEDs • Annual contract for CEO and chairman • 360° board evaluation disclosed to investors • Bonus arrangements disclosed and linked to TSR over >3 years
Responsive	• Formal investor access to NEDs • Formal/minuted review of investor input/contacts at each board meeting • Annual audit of investor sentiment

Source: Combined Code, Higgs Report, Cadbury Code and Myners Report.

of management quality to fund managers, potentially contributing to the value story. It would also allow fund managers with positions in a couple of analogous companies to draw clearer comparisons (Figure 11.5).

Executive compensation as a value lever

Where the rubber usually meets the road on the governance issue is over executive compensation. Over the past few years

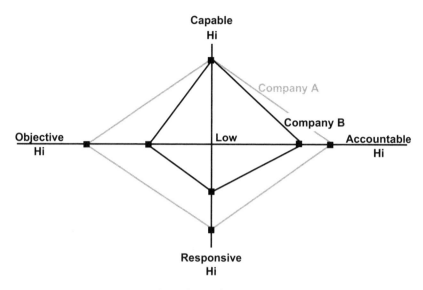

Figure 11.5 Benchmarking the quality of governance.

it has been on these grounds that most battles have been fought with fund managers – or to be more precise, over what have been perceived as excessive pay awards for low earnings per share (EPS) hurdles or even payoffs for failure. In a sense, it has become interpreted as the acid test of the power of the board over the CEO. A well-governed company controls run-away pay.

The bulk of executive rewards are, of course, not in cash. They are either in the form of options or share grants. And these awards are usually linked to some form of annual total shareholder returns or TSR. So, what is the problem? Surely, directly linking shareholder interests and those of the management team is eminent good logic? The closer the tie between management incentives and the goals of share-holders the better. Most quoted companies have followed that line of logic to the letter. Twenty years ago few firms had significant option schemes. Today, on average, 10% of large companies' shares are under option.

Until recently this was a wonderful arrangement for both management and shareholders. Options could be issued as part of the incentive package instead of cash. They had the benefit of usually only vesting over a number of years and hence tying the individual to the company and its market performance. They also did not hit the P&L until exercised, so that the compensation bill could in effect be deferred. And the dilution effect of options was often ignored by analysts by looking at EPS pre exercise of options.

This has now changed somewhat. In the USA at least, the difference between the strike price and current market value of options is increasingly expensed against the P&L annually, ensuring that companies will in future be far more sparing with their options grants. But, the link between shareprice and executive compensation has been fixed deep in the psyche. Most companies start out granting options that are linked to EPS, and later migrate towards options tied to total shareholder returns (i.e., shareprice plus dividends). They are easier to administer, easier to explain to share-holders, and more tangible for recipients. With the additional influence of compensation consultants, option-based schemes have become progressively more exotic. The two broad strands that have evolved are the LTIP and the STIP. The STIP, or short-term incentive plan, tends to target 1- to 2-year shareholder returns, and LTIPs 3- to 5-year returns. Both fit quite neatly with average executive tenure and also with the strategy-planning cycle.

So, what is wrong with this picture? The first problem emerges with the explicit link between compensation and shareprice. This means that managing shareholders to maximise shareprice potentially becomes more important than ensuring the business develops its long-term competitive position. Given that the average STIP and LTIP start paying out between 1 and 3 years, a strategy that maximises the shareprice over 2 to 3 years may well be a winning strategy. This means squeezing earnings per share any way it can be done. It means doing share buy-backs or acquisitions rather than investing in organic operations. The pressure to focus on shareprice can become overwhelming.

But, what happens with the inevitable correction? The answer is that in these circumstances any incentive scheme based on shareprice immediately collapses. This is precisely what has been happening with the value-based management (VBM) incentive structures embedded into so many companies over the past decade. Linking individual contributions to shareholder outcomes only works in a rising market or where the company is outperforming.

The principles of good governance summarised in this book suggest that the remuneration committee should be entirely independent and therefore control any excess remuneration. Perhaps more importantly, they need to shape executive compensation to reinforce a strategy of fair value rather than maximisation of TSR. STIPs and LTIPs should be geared to deliver when the company hits or exceeds the fair value targets set internally. This means that those targets have to be communicated to investors through the medium of the sell-side analyst based on explicit fair valuation parameters. This cements the link between investor and executive objectives but centred on a goal of staying in the fair value corridor.

Quality of management and the role of corporate branding

The logic of moving from an individualised concept of management quality to a more institutionalised notion of governance quality has important implications for the role of the corporate brand. In a situation where many active fund managers have precious little time for fundamental research, where they need clear messages, and where the company is seeking to shift emphasis onto the value story, the corporate brand has a clear role to play. This brings us once again back to what we can learn from the marketeers.

The notion that corporations have brands is now a well-established one. In 2000, as the stock market reached its peak, UK firms alone spent around £30m with branding consultants on this issue, followed by a slew of major renaming campaigns as brands were "refreshed". As belts have tightened and the frothiness evaporated, this spending has collapsed. But, it has also done so for a rational reason. Despite all the cash blown on promoting the corporate brand, there was very little evidence that companies were getting a lot out of it. Unless the corporate brand was synonymous with the customer brand (which it rarely was) there was little measurable revenue or margin benefit. With tougher times, marketing spend therefore got re-diverted to customer-facing brands.

Does this mean that the corporate brand has no place in the battle for share of the fund manager? Well, actually not. The problem with many of the major corporate branding campaigns is that they were not geared to fund managers as a primary audience. Whilst most included opinion research from this constituency, they actually employed the language and feel of mass consumer brands. This was hardly surprising as the consultants advising on them were usually of this heritage. Whilst it is hard to find clear evidence of the role of a corporate brand as a key influencer on fund manager opinion, it is logical to believe that, like any other human, fund managers respond to brands as indicators of value and drivers of aspiration – *"This feels like a quality proposition. I must have this one in my portfolio."* But, such brands have to respond to the needs of fund managers first and foremost.

It is likely that the corporate brand can be coopted in the management of fund manager perceptions. The important issue is what should the brand stand for and how are such qualities then communicated through this medium? How should the company emanate reliability, strength, probity and determination through the colour of its stationery, the look of its presentations and even its logo? The USPs of the company have to be researched with the value-determining investors on the register. Then, the bold decision has to be made that the primary audience of the corporate brand is this small constituency, not its mass of end customers, suppliers and other stakeholders. As a fair value lever, the primary opportunity held out by the corporate brand would appear to be to reinforce the notion of good governance as a counter-balance to the cult of individualism that is so often associated with shareprice maximisation.

And onwards . . .

The issue of how the company underpins its communications process with the "smell" of quality is an important but elusive affair. We have talked at length about the objective of counterbalancing the focus on the forecast with a more powerful value story. We have talked about the role of indirect signals of value rather than a barrage of direct mail shots and corporate advertising. How the notion of good management is embedded in this process is clearly an art. There is no right way to do it. It seems logical that in the balance between good governance and star management, the pursuit of fair value would incline the company towards the former. The corporate brand may be a useful tool in this process. But, as with so much of investor strategy, the question surfaces of who is going to coordinate these efforts? How can management decide how to play it? Who is going to do even the basic research of identifying value-determining investors such that efforts can be targeted appropriately? At the heart of the fair value proposition is a serious organisational challenge. That is where we go next.

Part Four
The Challenge of Managing for Fair Value

12

Managing a fair value strategy

The challenge of coordination

U NDERPINNING A COMPANY'S INTERACTION WITH THE capital markets is the investor relations function. Given the centrality of these sets of relationships to the fortunes of the management team and the viability of the strategy, you would assume that the Investor Relations (IR) function would be considered one of the most important at the corporate centre, one of its core pieces of value added to the entire group of companies under its control? The actual profile of the average IR function does not quite live up to that assumption.

Most FTSE companies employ a massive total of 3 people in the IR function (this compares with an average of 6 in the legal function, 18 in finance, 5 in HR and 4 in strategy). The average total direct payroll cost is around £200,000 or one-twentieth of the total payroll cost of the corporate centre. The annual budget, which is largely a communications budget, is around £2m: 40% of it accounted for by the logistics of fund managers' meetings, roadshows and materials; 30% of it accounted for by the annual report, interims and website. The balance is absorbed by the retention of a financial PR consultancy, broker and direct employee costs. Excluding the direct cost of the CEO's and CFO's time, the grand total investment is around 5% of central costs and less than one-seventh of a per cent of total group revenues. From our research the conclusion was clear. Most companies do not appear to invest in the IR process with the seriousness it deserves.

What about the professionals running the IR function? The IR director is typically an internal promotion. He or she usually migrate up through the corporation, typically coming from the strategy function, or from the finance group. They rarely ascend from line management. In a sense it is not an obvious career move as the role of IR director does not feed into any of the main avenues of career progression, such as director of strategy (which can then lead to being COO or even CEO), finance or line management itself. IR directors, unlike their strategy and finance counterparts, are rarely on the board. It is likely that historically some capable people have been a little suspicious of taking on the role. Since the role itself is only an invention of the past couple of decades, the fact that it is not tied into a professional trajectory is not surprising.

Increasingly, however, the IR director is being hired from outside, typically from apprenticeships in smaller listed companies where the IR function is less formalised. As a result, there is the gradual emergence of a professional class of IR directors who in the UK collectively amount to a community of several hundred. As an emerging professional body they are represented by the Investor Relations Society. But, what does this mean in practice? Are there a set of professional standards such as characterise other formal professions? Are there a set of established methodologies such as now underpin the corporate strategy process? Has there been well-documented, rigorous thinking about what constitutes best practice? Has IR evolved what could be called a set of strategic options to guide decision making?

The answer is no. The average IR function probably looks a little like the strategy function did 30 years ago – before McKinsey, Boston Consulting Group, Bain and a range of other consulting firms crystallised strategy into a profession. IR is increasingly acknowledged as an important function, but how exactly it should be done and how it creates value is still too often a matter of hit and miss. Too often it is something of an addendum to the personal agenda of the CEO and CFO, meaning it is largely focused on the logistics exercise of setting up endless meetings and preparing reports and publications, combined with responding to a daily avalanche of investor and analyst enquiries. The net effect of this is that there is little time for analysis of the register and little scope for proactive management of the relationship with active investors.

One expression of this lack of formalisation is that the IR function is almost never set direct performance targets. There is an appropriate analogy to be drawn with old-style marketing. Historically, marketing was charged with building the brand, raising consumer profile and getting the message out there. It was broadly accepted that it was more or less impossible to calculate return on investment for such activity. Companies had to content themselves with qualitative estimates of the impact of their efforts – consumer surveys, shelf share, share of voice. Then, marketing became more sophisticated. Direct marketing emerged as a statistically quantifiable discipline, quickly incorporating direct response TV, website campaigns and a range of response-driven activities. Now, performance can be measured and, combined with the explosion in market research, return on investment more reliably estimated.

What targets is IR set? Are there targets for investor churn? For investor recruitment? For establishing sources of core investor risk? Our research found an almost complete lack of measurement of outcomes. There was also little evidence of linking IR director compensation to favourable investor outcomes, other than the ubiquitous link in options schemes to shareprice maximisation. Interestingly, average IR director compensation appeared to weigh in a long way below that of the strategy director, and other peer-type professionals.

The absence of a culture of measurement emerges again in the lack of attention given to investor research. As we discussed in Chapter 3, most companies' knowledge of investors is a highly personalised affair. There is often little systematic understanding of what drives the behaviour of different fund managers and what are their triggers to investment and selling. Without a systematic evaluation of behaviours there is little ability to target IR activity.

The implicit assumption behind much IR activity is that all institutional fund managers can be treated alike. A single presentation forms the core of the investor round for the whole year. Part of this is a reflection of the regulatory regime which demands that no individual investor is given preferential access. But, part of it is usually down to fundamental absence of the knowledge necessary to target key investors and therefore to a lack of investor strategy.

Raising the game

The underpinning of any effective investor strategy is the ability to interrogate the share register. The IR director needs to demand enough resource in terms of data systems and manpower to regularly identify the value-determining investors on the register and to collate the information to understand and predict their behaviour. This process is likely to be underpinned by a screening tool, probably residing on the company's server. Coordinating the collection of insights from the various executives in contact with investors means that the IR group needs to formally and regularly debrief these executives. Whilst it would be expected that the house broker would help support this insight process, the know-how, the information resources and the analytical frameworks must reside with the company for a high level of expertise to be developed over time. This is particularly true when it comes to the calculation of the fair value corridor and determination of the company's position in it.

In order to gain targeted insight into value-determining investors, the IR director will need a direct and proactive approach with these fund managers. They will also need free reign to engage the analyst community in managing the valuation parameters being set and communicated to the markets. They will need effective control of the broker relationship in order to ensure all activities are tightly coordinated. They will also need a direct line into divisional line management to consolidate cashflows and both manage and interrogate the internal valuation emerging from this process.

In order to bring value levers to bear on these value-determining fund managers, the IR director will also need the power to act as the coordinating force behind a range of inputs, from the strategy-planning cycle to the annual forecasting cycle. They will have to make critical decisions about the communications mix, and about the content of messages. This will include critical decisions about the weighting and pitch of the value story, plus the evolution of the corporate brand. In short, they will be the coordinating force between executive management, the strategy team and the finance team in managing the investor base. Ultimately, it is they who will have to evaluate what actions the company needs to take to stay in the fair value corridor, producing the equivalent of the analysis illustrated in Table 12.1.

This all means that the role of the IR director and IR function will need to change. To be an effective decision maker, the IR director will need to be awarded status on par with the director of strategy. They might even be on par with the finance director and are likely to report directly to the CEO, with a dotted rather than direct line to the CFO. They may even be appointed to the board. The likelihood is that they will be hired from outside, as a mature professional in the field, although they may come from the broker community.

Table 12.1 Illustrative assessment of the impact of fair value levers

Action	Level of disruption	Potential value
Increased disclosure	◔	High
Financial signalling	◔	Medium/low
Revised capital structure	●	Medium
Strategic refocusing	●	Medium/high
Restructuring	●	Medium
Change of strategy	●	Medium/low
CEO change	●	Medium
NEDs strengthened	◑	High
Corporate downsized	◑	Medium
Revised incentives	◑	Medium/high
Targeting lead investors	○	High
Reduction of short-term expectations	◑	High
Refining the value story	○	High
Honing IR channel efficiency	○	Low/medium

Such a proposal would imply a revolution in the role of IR, the importance attached to it and in particular the status of the IR director. But none of this makes any sense if the only role of the IR function is to "sell" management to investors and to pursue the highest shareprice possible. A serious investment in IR, and the elevation of its status as a source of corporate value added, only makes sense if the objective of the company is pursuit of fair value. I hope this book has gone someway towards persuading you that this is the right course of action.

13

What to expect from the next decade

I N ORDER TO MANAGE THEIR RELATIONSHIP WITH INVESTORS effectively, any company has to understand how the competitive dynamics of the market for shares is likely to evolve in the near future. Is the battle for fund manager attention likely to get more competitive? Is the level of volatility going to remain high? Is indexation likely to increase and if so what should we do in response? Proper answers to these questions are essential to making the right decisions as regards investor strategy. I would argue that if a management team look clearly into the crystal ball the more convinced they will become that a fair value strategy is the only viable strategy they can adopt.

These sorts of questions are very familiar ones to the strategy folk. The tool commonly used by them to help find answers is Michael Porter's Five Forces.[1] The five-forces model proposes

---

[1] See Porter (1989).

that the level of competition in any market will not be determined by its level of growth or its size, as is habitually assumed. Rather, it will be the product of the power of buyers to drive down price and the ease with which they can change suppliers (known as switching costs). It will be driven by the power of suppliers to squeeze upstream margins and by the threat of new entrants who will increase the battle for market share. It will also be driven by the emergence of possible substitute products or services. These four drivers will determine the level of competition and hence likely profitability of an industry. There is a fifth force, government regulation, which in some industries also plays a strong hand in conditioning the level and nature of competition.

What about the market for stocks? All public companies compete in a market for institutional investors. In this market, fund managers could be thought of as customers who have their own switching costs. Companies also have critical suppliers – the brokers and analysts that support the stock. They also suffer the threat of new entrants as competitor firms' IPOs come to market, and new powerful players emerge, typically as a result of consolidation. They also suffer the threat of substitution, as alternative objects of investment emerge, including instruments that are not equities at all, such as derivatives. Regulation also plays its role, enforcing standards of disclosure and raising limits on director liability. Depending on how these variables evolve over time, so the level of competition a company experiences in attracting fund manager attention will shift dramatically.

If you reflect on the past decade up to 2001, this analysis tells a clear tale. During this period, demand for stocks increased dramatically, driven by the surge in investment by individuals in investment and mutual funds. This was in turn compounded by a shift by pension and insurance funds more heavily into equities. As a result the competition for stocks increased and buyer power decreased. During the same period, the supply side also altered dramatically. By 1995 the investment-banking business had consolidated into the hands of seven or eight bulge bracket firms. It was no longer an environment of fragmented, local specialist providers. The large players combined capital depth, enabling them to take principal risk, with huge distribution power. This allowed them to raise fees. But, more importantly, it meant that they had more power to drive the stock value of their clients. In this case rising supplier power probably helped propel an acceleration of stock prices.

The level of new entrants was dramatic, with an average of almost 100 significant new companies coming to market in each major market per year. Many of these offered the promise of far higher growth prospects than mature stocks. As a result they sucked investor cash out of more traditional businesses with lower growth trajectories. The result was a relative de-rating of mature, "old-economy" businesses. There was also a surge of interest in substitute investments other than holding shares. These principally took the form of derivatives which allowed an investor to go short or long on a stock without actually holding it, hence tying up a fraction of the capital. As a result firms found their shareprice being driven by funds who didn't actually hold shares in a conventional sense and who they could not influence. The world had suddenly got more complex and demanding. The net impact of all this was temporarily positive in terms of general total shareholder returns (TSRs), but also intensely volatile. It was a period which fundamentally destabilised the share registers and strategies of many well-established businesses.

This is all old history. But, roll the clock forward. Things look very different. As I write this book, customer demand has declined. Many pension and insurance funds are reducing their exposure to equities, and mutual funds are experiencing considerable contraction as individual investors withdraw to less volatile assets. The supply side has also altered. Although consolidation is continuing, the power of the bulge bracket firms to set price has diminished. The credibility of the sell-side analyst function has been put in some doubt. The broker as the arbiter of value is under increased regulatory pressure. The substitute asset classes which so plagued shareholder registers in the previous decade persist in wreaking their havoc. Hedge funds, the principle employers of derivatives, have actually benefited from the volatility of the markets, achieving better returns even than private equity firms. Meanwhile, the volume of new entrants has dried up, as the credibility of high-growth hi-tech stories has evaporated. Suddenly, mature "old-economy" stocks and sectors are back in fashion.

So, overall, the environment is challenging but perhaps also more manageable as a result of the decline in supplier power, the diminishing threat of new entrants and an increased comfort with value stocks. This is the aggregate view. The relevant market for an individual company is likely to share some of the same characteristics but will also have its peculiarities. For most companies the relevant investor market will be dictated by the sector they are classified in and also the indexes they are included in. But, if I were to be forced to look into the great crystal ball, these are the big trends I would see evolving:

(1) The customers

- The shareholder challenge is due to get a lot more complex, rather than simpler.

    o Non-conventional investors, such as hedge funds, are likely to increase their role rather than diminish, propelled by the onward advance of derivatives.

    o Cross-border investment will grow rapidly, producing more diverse registers, with less clear relationship lines.

    o Volatility of holdings will increase as fund managers come under ever-greater competitive pressures to maximise annual returns and mandate cycles tighten.

    o There will be an increasing impersonalisation of the investment process, making old-style relationship management a tough proposition.

(2) The suppliers

- The sell side in general will weaken as a distribution force.

○ The sell-side analyst will be increasingly unbundled from the commission-based activity of the investment banks and sell advice to institutional subscribers. This will drive a less comfortable, more critical style of intermediary. Pressure will be brought to dampen marketing-style over-rating of client stocks.

○ The buy-side analyst is likely to assume greater prominence. This will mean the old relationship-based process between company and fund manager will diminish in favour of a more analytically based approach.

○ The broker will no longer be able to justify the cost of detailed register analysis to support its clients, and their power in the distribution change will shift.

(3) The substitutes

• Substitution will grow as a determinant of competition.

○ The volume of substitutes to ownership of underlying shares will continue to increase through growth in derivatives, making registers more complex to analyse and movements harder to predict.

○ Alternative asset classes, such as private equity, will continue to grow.

○ A range of investors will seek more secure assets classes, such as debt and property.

(4) The new entrants

- The process of new entrants will, as always, follow the economic cycle.

  o New issues and IPOs will not return to former levels for quite a while at the large end.

(5) Government policy

- Regulatory pressure will continue to grow.

  o Demands for disclosure will increase, along with more involved managerial examination and obligation.

  o Pension fund trustees obligations will increase.

It's the opinion of this author that the net effect of these trends will be a highly competitive market for companies, but one in which fair value strategies will gain increased credence v. shareprice maximisation strategies. In this evolving world for stocks, the Investor Relations (IR) director will emerge to take the mantel of intellectual authority that has been carried for two decades by the strategy group. IR will emerge as a board-level function, reporting directly to the CEO rather than through finance. The age of IR is upon us. If you don't believe me, just do the market analysis for yourself.

Bibliography

Alessandri, T.M and Bettis, R.A. (2003) Surviving the bulls and the bears: Robust strategies and shareholder wealth. *Long Range Planning*, **36**, 13–35.

Barberis, N., Shleifer, A. and Vishny, R. (1998). A model of investor sentiment. *Journal of Financial Economics*, **49**, 307–343.

Barsky, R. and De Long, J.B. (1993) Why does the stock market fluctuate? *Quarterly Journal of Economics*, **108**, 291–311.

Bernard, V. (1992) Stock price reactions to earnings announcements. In: R. Thaler (ed.), *Advances in Behavioural Finance*. New York: Russell Sage Foundation.

Bernard, V. and Thomas, J.K. (1990) Evidence that stock prices do not fully reflect the implications of current earnings for future earnings. *Journal of Accounting and Economics*, **13**, 305–341.

Booth, T. (2003) Other people's money. *The Economist*, July 5th.

Boston Consulting Group (2001) *Dealing with Investors' Expectations: A Global Study of Company Valuations and Their Strategic Implications* (BCG report). Boston: Boston Consulting Group.

Brealey, R.A. and Myers, S.C. (1996) *Principles of Corporate Finance* (5th edn). New York: McGraw-Hill.

Bromiley, P. and James-Wade, S. (2003) Putting rational blinders behind us: Behavioural understandings of finance and strategic management. *Long Range Planning*, **36**, 37–48.

Chapman, C. (1998) *How the Stock Markets Work* (6th edn). London: Century Business Books.

Chen, N., Roll, R. and Ross, S. (1986) Economic forces and the stock market. *Journal of Business*, **59**, 383–403.

Chopra, N., Lakonishok, J. and Ritter, J. (1992). Measuring abnormal performance: Do stocks overreact? *Journal of Financial Economics*, **31**, 235–268.

Clark, W.M. (1995) *How the City of London Works* (4th edn). London: Sweet & Maxwell.

Coombes, P. and Watson, M. (2000) Three surveys on corporate governance. *The McKinsey Quarterly*, **4**.

Coyne, K.P. and Witter, J.W. (2002a) Taking the mystery out of investor behaviour. *Harvard Business Review*, September.

Coyne, K.P. and Witter, J.W. (2002b) What makes your stock price go up and down. *The McKinsey Quarterly*, **2**.

Daniel, K., Hirshleifer, D. and Subrahmanyam, A. (1998) Investor psychology and security market under- and overreactions. *Journal of Finance*, **53**, 1839–1885.

De Bondt, W.F.M. and Thaler, R. (1985) Does the stock market overreact? *Journal of Finance*, **40**, 793–805.

De Bondt, W.F.M. and Thaler, R. (1987) Further evidence on investor overreaction and stock market seasonality. *Journal of Finance*, **42**, 557–581.

Dreman, D. and Berry, M. (1995) Overreaction, underreaction, and the low-p/e effect. *Financial Analysts Journal*, **51**, 21–30.

Eccles, R.G., Hertz, R.H., Keegan, M.E. and Phillips, D.M.H. (2001) *The Value Reporting Revolution Moving Beyond the Earnings Game*. Chichester, UK: John Wiley & Sons.

Endlich, L. (1999) *Goldman Sachs: The Culture of Success*. Boston: Little & Brown.

Fama, E. (1965) The behaviour of stock market prices. *Journal of Business*, **38**, 34–106.

Felton, R.F. and Watson, M. (2002) Change across the board. *The McKinsey Quarterly*, **4**.

Geisst, C.R. (1997) *Wall Street: A History*. New York: Oxford University Press.

Golding, T. (2001) *The City: Inside the Great Expectation Machine*. London: Financial Times/Prentice Hall.

Gompers, P. and Metrick, A. (1999) Institutional investors and equity prices (Mimeo). Cambridge, MA: Harvard University Press.

Goodman, G. [Adam Smith] (1968) *The Money Game*. New York: McGraw-Hill.

Grossman, S. and Stiglitz, J. (1980) On the impossibility of information-ally efficient markets. *American Economic Review*, **70**, 393–408.

Hampden-Turner, C. and Trompenaars, F. (1993) *The Seven Cultures of Capitalism*. London: Piatkus Books.

Haspeslagh, P., Noda, T. and Boulos, F. (2001) Managing for value: It's not just about the numbers. *Harvard Business Review*, **7222**, July/August.

Healy, P.M., Hutton, A.P. and Palepu, K.G. (1999) Stock performance and intermediation changes surrounding sustained increases in disclosure. *Contemporary Accounting Research*, **16**(3), Fall, 485–520.

Hermes Focus Asset Management (2002) *UK Shareholder Programme Case Studies* (August). Hermes Focus Asset Management.

Higgs, D. (2003) *Review of the Role and Effectiveness of Non-executive Directors* (January). London: Department of Trade & Industry.

Jensen, M. (1978) Some anomalous evidence regarding market efficiency. *Journal of Financial Economics*, **6**, 95–101.

Koller, T.M. (2003) Numbers investors can trust. *The McKinsey Quarterly*, **3**.

Lakonishok, J., Shleifer, A., Thaler, R. and Vishny, R. (1991) Window dressing by pension fund managers. *American Economic Review Papers and Proceedings*, **81**, 227–231.

Lawler, E.E. III, Benson, G.S., Finegold, D.L. and Conger, J.A. (2002) Corporate boards: Keys to effectiveness. *Organizational Dynamics*, **30**(4), 310–324.

Littlewood, J. (1998) *The Stock Market: 50 Years of Capitalism at Work*. London: Financial Times/Prentice Hall..

Lubatkin, M.H., Schulze, W.S., McNulty, J.J. and Yeh, T.D. (2003) But will it raise my share price? New thoughts about an old question. *Long Range Planning*, **36**, 81–91.

Miller, M. and Modigliani, F. (1961) Dividend policy, growth, and the valuation of shares. *Journal of Business*, **34**, 411–433.

Nisbet, M. (1994) Segmenting the City. *Long Range Planning*, **27**(1), 154–156.

O'Sullivan, N., Diacon, P. and Stephen, R. (2003) Board composition and performance in life insurance companies. *British Journal of Management*, **14**, 115–129.

Porter, M. (1989) *Competitive Strategy*. New York: Free Press.

Sanders, G.W.M. and Boivie, S. (2004) Sorting things out: Valuation of new firms in uncertain markets. *Strategic Management Journal*, **25**, 167–186.

Scharfstein, D. and Stein, J. (1990) Herd behaviour and investment. *American Economic Review*, **80**, 465–489.

Shleifer, A. (2000) *Inefficient Markets: An Introduction to Behavioural Finance*. New York: Oxford University Press.

Soros, G. (1998) *The Crisis of Global Capitalism*. New York: Public Affairs.

Thomas, A., Gietzmann, M. and Shyla, A. (2002) Winning the competition for capital. *European Business Forum*, **9**, Spring.

Weetman, P. and Beattie, A. (1999) *Corporate Communications: Views of Institutional Investors and Lenders*. Institute of Chartered Accountants of Scotland.

Index

5-year projections 901, 104–7, 228

Aberdeen 127
absolute-value measures 841–17
account management 66–7, 74, 77, 136–46,
    227–9
accountability issues 204–20
accounting processes 106, 164–85, 192–3,
    208, 229, 232, 237
accrual-based earnings 84–5, 164
acquisitions *see* mergers ...
action steps 158
active investors 4–5, 38–40, 45–6, 51, 56–63,
    99–100, 119–34, 176, 194–200, 227–9
    see also value-determining shareholders
ad hoc elements, investor communications
    189–90
advisors, system overview 26–7
agents, system overview 26–7
AGMs *see* annual general meetings
amortisation 84–5, 109, 116
analysts
    benefits 34, 35–6
    biases 29–37, 39, 82, 117, 170, 196
    failings 234
    forecasts 29–37, 41, 82, 89–90, 150–1,
        174–8, 196, 199–200, 234–5
    future prospects 235–6
    investment bankers 30–1, 34, 236
    knowledge benefits 34, 150–1, 174, 227–8
    lead analysts 150–1, 181–4
    motivation cycles 31–2
    notes 29–37, 82, 161, 189–91, 195, 212
    roles 26, 29–36, 82, 150–1, 174–5, 196,
        234–6

sell-side analysts 26, 29–37, 74, 82, 89–90,
    102–3, 145, 150–1, 169–70, 174–5, 181–4,
    196, 199–200, 234–7
statistics 301
announcements 78–9, 98–9, 159–62, 187–200
annual forecasts 149–62, 175–8, 199–200
annual general meetings (AGMs) 34, 48–9,
    126, 145, 187–90
annual reports 34, 164–5, 187–200, 212,
    223–4
annual statements 173
arbitrage opportunities 12, 21, 44, 59–60, 129
ARM 152
Asia 207
Audit committees 208–9, 211, 214
audits 127–8, 167–85, 208–20
    see also accounting ...

Bacon and Woodrow 53
Bain 225
balance sheets 106, 16785
barriers to entry 173, 232–7
BCG *see* Boston Consulting Group
bear markets 23–5, 38, 95
behavioural finance 24–5, 39–40, 48, 135–46
benchmarks 138–9, 175, 178–85, 212–20
beta, CAPM 87–116
biases 22–5, 27–40, 82, 117, 170
blockholders, directional traders 62, 143–6
boards 18–19, 78–80, 205–20, 224, 237
    see also management
bonuses, management 41–2
Boston Consulting Group (BCG) 102, 107,
    225

brands 155–6, 169, 173–5, 179–85, 188–9,
  199, 218–20, 225–6
break-up analysis 112
brokers 2, 45, 11, 13–14, 26–36, 77, 102–3,
  122, 128, 144–6, 190–200, 227–8, 232–7
  see also house brokers; sell-side analysts
  background 4–5, 11, 13–14, 26–36, 102–3,
    144–6, 227–8, 234–7
  benefits 34, 35–6
  biases 25, 27–37, 39, 82, 117, 170
  commissions 29–31
  failings 28, 234
  future prospects 235–6
  mission 26–36
  motivation cycles 31–2
  power issues 33–4, 102–3, 151
  roles 27–33, 34, 102–3, 144–6, 236–7
budgeting processes 100–6, 111, 117, 151–2,
  188–9, 223–4, 228
Buffett, Warren 154
bulge-bracket firms 233–7
bull markets 23–5, 37, 103
'bundled' trading commissions 29–30
buy-backs 16, 78–80, 139, 157–62, 196–200,
  217–18
  see also fair value levers
buy-side analysts 32, 34, 37, 121–2, 236
  see also fund managers
buyers, Porter's Five Forces model 232–7

Cadbury Code 207, 212–14
CAPEX *see* capital expenditure
capital
  cost of capital 42–3, 73–80, 87–116, 179–84
  structure changes 78–9, 159–62, 196–200,
    229
capital asset pricing model (CAPM) 22, 86,
  87–115
capital expenditure (CAPEX) 72, 86, 101,
  108–11, 116, 179–84
capital-raising processes 12–13
  see also rights issues
CAPM *see* capital asset pricing model
cash cows 109–11
cashflow measures 22, 25, 84–117, 174–8,
  179–84, 196–200, 228
cashflow statements 167–85
CEOs *see* chief executive officers
CFOs *see* chief financial officers
CFROI 84–5
chairmen, CEOs 208–9, 214
changes
  management 3, 19, 24, 45–6, 72, 78–9,
    158–62, 171, 196–200, 202–3, 209–10,
    229
  strategy 78–9, 158–62, 196–200, 204–5, 229
chief executive officers (CEOs) 15, 9–19, 33,
  41–6, 61, 63–5, 71, 101–2, 121–2, 171,
  177, 188, 191, 201–15, 229, 237
  see also management
  chairmen 208–9, 214
  charismatic CEOs 203–5, 212
  disclosures 163–4, 171
  'feel' judgements 121–2, 124, 191

non-executive directors 209–11
  presentation techniques 188
  qualities 201–5, 212
  roles 1–2, 13–14, 18–19, 33, 41, 63–5, 71,
    101–2, 121–2, 177, 188, 191, 201–15, 237
  shareprice maximisation crusades 2–5,
    9–19, 41–6, 71, 202–3, 212
  tenure statistics 3, 19, 24, 201–2, 229
  track records 202–5
chief financial officers (CFOs) 1–2, 4–5,
  13–14, 61, 63–5, 101–2, 121–2, 136, 191,
  201–15
  IR 4–5, 101–2, 191
  roles 1–2, 13–14, 63–5, 101–2, 121–2, 136,
    191
Chinese walls, investment bankers 29
churn, investors 4, 45–6
The City 2, 61
clients *see* customer ...
closet indexes 55–7, 122–6, 137–8, 170
CNN 203
Coke 2
Combined Code 207–8, 212–14
commentators 195
commissions 13, 28–31, 57, 141–2
communications 18–19, 34, 48–9, 63–6, 74,
  78–80, 101, 103–4, 124, 141–6, 156–62,
  187–200, 223–9
  see also fair value levers
  active investors 194–200
  ad hoc elements 189–90
  budgeting processes 101, 223–4
  channels 74, 78–80, 156–62, 187–200
  coopting practices 141–6, 190–200
  customisation issues 191–5
  direct communications 78–80, 124, 156–62,
    189–200
  effectiveness assessments 191–2
  indirect communications 78–80, 156–62,
    195–200
  marketing 188–93, 200
  mix 199–200
  simplicity benefits 198–9
  strategy 193–200, 223–9
  types 78–9, 124, 141–2, 156–62, 189–200
  value-determining shareholders 156–62,
    194–200, 227–9
companies 267, 637
  see also investors
compensation
  management 13, 41–3, 72, 78–9, 100–1,
    159–62, 196–200, 208–20, 226
  value levers 214–18
competition, Porter's Five Forces model
  231–7
competitive advantage, disclosures 165
competitor analysis 144–6, 173
composite sheets, investor profiles 139–40
composition, boards 18–19, 78–80, 205–6,
  224, 237
conservatism, fund managers 53–8, 103
coopting practices, value-determining
  shareholders 141–6, 190–200

coordination needs 4–5, 18–19, 79–80,
189–62, 187–200, 220, 223–9
core competencies 5, 16, 158
core-style category, account management
138–46
corporate brands 218–20
see also brands
corporate costs 112–13, 145
corporate governance *see* governance issues
corporate strategy *see* strategy
corrections 14–17, 21–5, 44–5, 158
corridors *see* fair value corridor
cost of capital 42–3, 73–80, 87–117, 179–84
cost-cutting pressures, fund managers 39–40,
123–4
cost/benefit analysis, disclosures 183–4,
229
costs
corporate costs 112–13, 145
fund managers 39–40, 54–5, 123–4, 141–2
imperfect markets 14–15, 17, 43–6
IR 145, 223–4
low disclosures 163–4, 169–71
misvaluation traps 14–15, 17, 43–6, 72, 84,
116–17
premiums 14–15, 17, 43–6, 83–4, 116–17
short-termism 14–15, 17, 43–6, 71–2
crib sheets 123–4
CRM *see* customer relationship management
customer acquisitions/retentions, non-
financial performance measures 155–6,
169, 173–5, 179–84
customer relationship management (CRM)
192, 204
customers
see also investors; shareholder ...
Porter's Five Forces model 232–7
customisation issues, IR processes 191–5
cyclical inevitability 3–4, 12–19, 23–5, 41,
43–6, 72, 129, 171

data points 24–5, 48, 123–5
databases, account management 136–7
DCF *see* discounted cashflow analysis
debt issuance 28–9, 236
decay functions, operating margins 109–10
departmental conflicts, fair value levers 79,
161–2
depreciation 84–5, 109–11, 116
deregulated markets 11, 207–8
derivatives 60, 62–3, 131, 232–7
see also hedge funds; options
direct communications, concepts 78–80, 124,
156–62, 189–200
direct costs, fair value strategy 145
direct marketing 189, 192–3, 226
directional traders 40, 47–8, 58–63, 76–80,
119–34, 143–6, 194–200, 227–9
see also value-determining shareholders
directors
see also management
governance issues 207–20
IR 103, 117, 136, 187–200, 224–9, 237

non-executive directors 78–80, 159–62,
190–200, 201–2, 207–20, 229
share-dealing practices 157
disclosures 18–19, 22, 49, 74–80, 152–62,
164–85, 192–3, 229, 232, 237
see also fair value levers
accounting processes 164–85, 192–3, 229,
232, 237
background 18–19, 22, 49, 74–80, 152–62,
164–85, 192–3, 229, 232, 237
benefits 165–75, 178–85, 229
CEOs 163–4, 171
competitive advantage 165
cost/benefit analysis 183–4
future prospects 237
gaps 178–85
low disclosures 163–4, 169–71
mindset changes 171–5
mistrust issues 170–1, 185
non-financial performance measures 169,
173–6, 179–84
performance measures 164, 169, 173–85
priorities 176–7, 180–1
returns links 178
risk /reward analysis 183–4
value-determining shareholders 178–85
discount rates 88–9, 114–15
discounted cashflow analysis (DCF) 22, 25,
84–5, 88–9, 107
discounts, undervalued shares 44–5, 73–4, 83,
116–17, 158–60
disruptive value levers, concepts 160–2
divestiture focus 16–17, 73, 158, 179–85
dividend yield 97–8
dividends 16–17, 78–9, 97–8, 157–62, 196–200
see also fair value levers
divisional levels, cashflow measures 111–12,
116–17, 174
dot.com revolution 25, 233–4
Dow Jones Industrial Average 3, 10

earnings measures 13, 16, 23, 41, 91–9, 106,
150–1, 152–3, 157, 168–70, 175, 177, 197,
215–16
earnings per share (EPS) 13, 41, 94–8, 150–1,
157, 169–70, 177, 215–16
earnings-smoothing practices 168–9
EBIT 92
EBITA 92
EBITDA 84–6, 92
economic value added (EVA) 42–3, 84–5
education issues, fund managers 182
emails 189
Enron 43, 167, 206
enterprise value, concepts 73–80, 102, 108,
115–17, 180–1
EPS *see* earnings per share
equity divisions, investment bankers 28–30
European investors 188, 207
EVA *see* economic value added
executive 5, 18–19, 79–80, 161–2, 187–200,
228–9
see also chief ...; management

exit consequences, indexes 10–11, 45–6,
55–6, 138
expectation-setting processes 149–62, 174–8
extreme outcomes, biases 25

fair value
assessment processes 74, 76, 96–117, 228–9
budgeting processes 104–6, 111, 117
concepts 1–5, 15–16, 18–19, 46, 67, 71–80,
104–5, 205–20
definition 75
levers assessment processes 74, 77–80,
149–200
principles 76–80, 106–17
process overview 73–80, 109
rules 103–6
strategy 4–5, 18–19, 46, 67, 71–80, 100–17,
145–6, 147–220, 231–7
value maximisation alternative 19, 237
fair value corridor
acceptable limits 75–6, 99–100, 116–17
account management step 74, 77, 136–46
concepts 75–80, 96–117, 158–62, 171–5,
227–9
defining step 74, 76, 96–117, 228–9
investor-profiling step 74, 77, 135–46,
226–9
investor-screening step 74, 76–7, 119–34,
145, 180, 227–9
levers assessment step 74, 77–80, 149–200
non-disruptive value levers 158–62
steps overview 75–80
value-determining investors identification
step 74, 76–7, 119–34, 135–46, 180, 219,
227–9
fair value levers
categories 74, 78–80, 156–62
concepts 74, 77–80, 149–200, 212–20,
228–9
coordination needs 79–80, 159–62,
187–200, 223–9
departmental conflicts 79, 161–2
governance issues 212–14, 220
non-disruptive value levers 158–62
types 158–62
'feel' judgements, management 121–2, 124,
191
fiduciary duties 39–40, 117, 208–9
finance function 5, 18–19, 77–80, 161–2,
187–200, 224, 228–9
financial markets
concepts 1–5, 21–46,
101–2, 117, 121–2, 136, 170, 232–3
market value 75–80, 84, 96–117, 171–5
perfect/imperfect markets 21–5, 40–6, 73,
95
system overview 26–7
financial metrics, disclosure gaps 179–85
financial models, valuations 107–17
Financial Services Authority (FSA) 164, 207
Financial Times 92–3
Five Forces model, competition 231–7
Forbes 203

forecasts 29–37, 41, 82, 86–117, 149–62, 170,
174–8, 196, 199–200, 228–9
see also predictions
5-year projections 90–1, 104–7, 228
analysts 29–37, 41, 82, 89–91, 150–1,
174–8, 196, 199–200, 234–5
cashflow measures 86–117, 174–8, 179–84,
228
concepts 86–117, 149–62, 174–8, 196, 199–
200, 228–9
dampening effects 115–16
empowerment 105–6
expectation-setting processes 149–62,
174–8
human nature 90–1, 102–3, 115–16
over-optimistic forecasts 90–1, 102–3,
115–16, 151–2, 170, 196
pushed-down forecasts 105–6
Fortune 500 42
free cashflows 84–117, 179–84, 196–200
Friedman, Milton 21
FSA *see* Financial Services Authority
FTSE 100 3, 10, 28, 87, 91, 192, 209
FTSE 250 2, 28, 87, 164
FTSE All Share Actuarial Index 36, 56
fund managers 2–5, 11–19, 24–40, 45–6,
47–67, 119–34, 136–46, 205–20, 232–7
see also investors
account management 66–7, 74, 77, 136–46,
227–9
active investors 4–5, 38–40, 45–6, 51,
56–63, 99–100, 119–34, 136–46, 176
background 2–5, 11–19, 24–40, 45–6, 47–67,
119–34, 136–46, 205–20, 232–7
behaviour prediction processes 74, 77, 121–
34, 135–46, 149, 226–7
biases 38–40, 117, 170
CEO roles 2, 33, 63–5, 71, 121–2, 201–15
CFO roles 101–2, 121–2, 136
complexity issues 49–53
conservatism 53–8, 103
corporate brands 219
costs 39–40, 54–5, 123–4, 141–2
directional traders 40, 47–8, 58–63, 76–80,
119–34, 194–200, 227–9
education issues 182
future prospects 235–7
hedge funds 19, 38, 50–1, 59–63, 124, 129,
133, 141, 143–4, 176, 234–5
herd instincts 39–40, 48, 62, 76–80, 119–34
independence problems 28
indexation trends 11, 38–40, 51–63, 71,
122–6, 231
leverage issues 39, 123–4
location factors 63–4
loyal/unloyal investors 63–5
mandate lifetimes 54–5, 128–34, 138–9
market capitalisations 49, 55–6
meetings 34, 48–9, 63–6, 120–2, 136, 141–
2, 145, 173, 187–200, 209–12, 225
minorities 124–8
motivations 135–46
net changes in individual holdings 130–4,
160

fund managers (*cont.*)
  passive investors 36–40, 45–6, 51, 55–7,
    122–34
  performance measures 36–40, 53–8, 121–2
  pooled funds 52–3
  profiles 57, 74, 77, 135–46
  relationships 2, 29–30, 33–6, 40, 63–5, 75,
    119–34, 165, 201–20, 223–9
  roles 36–40, 235–7
  shake-out 17
  shares-traded figures 129–34, 160
  short-termism effectors 3, 11–19, 35–6,
    40–6, 54–6, 58–63, 171, 175
  size issues 39–40, 49, 55, 63–4, 119–21,
    123, 128–9, 142
  statistics 24, 36–40, 49–67, 119–29, 141–2
  strategy 56, 120–1, 141
  system overview 26
  tenure statistics 24, 50, 54, 141–2
  types 26–7
fundamental analysis, limited opportunities
    39, 81–2
fundamental performance
  concepts 9–10, 11–14, 16, 18–19, 38–9,
    73–80, 81–117
  indexation behaviour 38–9
  shareprice maximisation contrasts 9–10,
    11–12, 13–14, 16, 73–80
fundamental value concepts 39, 75–80,
    81–117
  market value 75–80, 84, 96–117
  strategy processes 100–1
future performance potential
  see also fundamental performance
  concepts 9–10, 73–80, 86–117, 149–62,
    168–9, 173–5
  non-financial performance measures 155–6,
    169, 173–6, 179–84
future prospects 231–7
future volatility, historical volatility 87–8,
    114–15, 175–6

gaming tactics 15–16, 19, 182–4
GDP 91, 108–9
gearing figures 98
Gillette 35, 154
Gilts 87–8
goals 9–19, 71, 113
good governance, concepts 204–20, 237
goodwill valuations 167
governance issues 161, 192–3, 204–20, 237
  concepts 161, 192–3, 204–20, 237
  critique 209–15, 237
  non-executive directors 201–2, 207–20, 229
  Reports 207–8, 212–14
  self-regulations 208–20
  value levers 212–14, 220
growth stocks, overvaluations 30–1

hedge funds 19, 38, 50–1, 59–63, 124, 129,
    133, 141, 143–4, 176, 234–5
Henderson 127
herd instincts 39–40, 48, 62, 76–80, 119–34
Hermes Focus 127, 143

Higgs Report 207–8, 212–14
historical measures 86–90, 114–15, 156,
    168–9, 173, 175–6
historical volatility 87–8, 114–15, 175–6
  see also volatility honesty issues 203
'hot' sectors 11–12
house brokers 2, 13, 27–36, 77, 102–3, 122,
    128, 144–6, 151–2, 190–200, 227–8, 232–7
  see also brokers power issues 33–4, 102–3,
    128, 151
  roles 27–33, 34, 102–3, 122, 128, 144–6,
    151–2, 227–8
HP 2, 35
HR management 1, 13

imperfect markets 14–15, 17, 21–5, 40–6, 73,
    95
in-house management, insurance companies
    36–40, 51
incentive schemes, management 13, 41–3,
    78–9, 100–1, 159–62, 196–200, 216–20,
    226
indexation trends 11, 38–40, 51–63, 71,
    122–34, 231
indexes 2–3, 10, 36–40, 51–3, 54–63, 92–3,
    122–6
  see also Dow ...; FTSE ...; S&P ...
  closet indexes 55–7, 122–6, 137–8, 170
  exit consequences 10–11, 45–6, 54–6, 138
  importance 10, 36–40, 54–7, 92–3, 122–6
  market caps 10, 37–40, 55–6
  relative value measures 92–9, 152
indirect communications, concepts 78–80,
    156–62, 195–200
indirect costs, fair-value strategy 145
industry/competitive data, disclosure gaps
    179–85
inflation traps, expectation-setting processes
    154–6
influencibility-level category, account
    management 137–46
information access 21–2, 34, 37, 47–50, 136,
    145–6, 171–5, 179–84, 227–9
  see also disclosures; shareholder registers
initial public offers (IPOs) 232, 237
innovations, non-financial performance
    measures 155–6, 169, 173–5, 179–84
institutional investors 2–5, 11–19, 26–8,
    33–46, 47–67, 74, 77, 99–100, 119–34,
    135–46, 149, 176, 226–9, 232–7
  see also fund managers; insurance
    companies; investment trusts; pension
    funds; unit trusts
insurance companies 26–7, 29–30, 36–40,
    50–67, 176, 233–4
  see also institutional investors
integrity issues 203
Intel 2, 154
interim results 34, 224
intermediary market, system overview 26–7
internal valuations *see* self-valuations
Internet 48, 165, 187–200, 224, 226
Interpublic 94

investment bankers 12–13, 28–36, 233, 236–7
  analysts 30–1, 34, 236
  commissions 28–31
  debt issuance 28–9
  equity divisions 28–30
  M&As 28, 30
  rights issues 28–9
  roles 28–30, 236
investment consultants, roles 52, 53
investment trusts 26–7, 50–1
  see also institutional investors
investment triggers category, account
  management 138–46
investor relations (IR) 2–5, 18–19, 22–3, 34,
    40, 48–9, 74–5, 89, 101–3, 117, 136, 145,
    156–7, 177, 187–200, 223–9, 237
  annual reports 34, 187–200, 223–4
  compensation 226
  concepts 2–5, 18–19, 22–3, 34, 40, 48–9, 89,
    101–3, 117, 136, 145, 156–7, 177,
    187–200, 223–9, 237
  coordinating role 4–5, 18–19, 34, 79–80,
    117, 161–2, 187–200, 223–9
  costs 145, 223–4
  customisation issues 191–5
  directors 103, 117, 136, 187–200, 224–9,
    237
  future prospects 237
  marketing analogies 188–93, 200, 225–6
  outsourcing 5
  performance issues 225–6
  professional standards 225
  staff 103, 117, 136, 187–200, 224–5, 237
  statistics 223–4
  tactical processes 191
Investor Relations Society 225
investors 1–5, 18–19, 22–3, 26–7, 29–30, 33–6,
    40, 45–67, 74–5, 77, 119–34, 136–46, 165,
    201–20, 223–9, 232–7
  see also fund managers; shareholder ...
  active investors 4–5, 38–40, 45–6, 51,
    56–63, 99–100, 119–34, 136–46, 176
  audits 127–8
  behaviour prediction processes 74, 77,
    121–34, 135–46, 149, 226–7
  CEO roles 1–2, 63–5, 71, 121–2, 201–15
  CFO roles 101–2, 121–2, 136
  churn 4, 45–6
  concepts 1–5, 26–7, 33–6, 40, 45–9
  exits 45–6, 64–5, 138
  expectation-setting processes 149–62,
    174–8
  future prospects 235–7
  loyal/unloyal investors 63–5
  meetings 34, 48–9, 63–6, 120–2, 136,
    141–2, 145, 151, 173, 187–200, 209–12,
    225
  passive investors 36–40, 45–6, 51, 55–7,
    122–34
  perceptions 4–5, 45–6, 66, 77–80
  Porter's Five Forces model 232–7
  profiles 57, 74, 77, 135–46
  retail investors 48–9, 57
  segmentation uses 52, 66–7

statistics 24, 36–40, 48–67, 119–29, 141–2
substitute investors 77–8, 143–6
system overview 26–7
IPOs see initial public offers
IR see investor relations

journals 195
'jungle drums' 125–6

knowledge 34, 73–80, 116–17, 125–6, 136,
    150–1, 174–5, 227–8

Latin America 207
lead analysts 150–1, 180–4
  see also analysts
lead investors 124–8
leverage issues, fund managers 39, 123–4
Leverhulme, Lord 71
levers–assessment step, fair–value corridor
    74, 77–80, 149–200
location factors, fund managers 63–4
long-term incentive plans (LTIPs) 42, 216–17
long-term valuation 2–3, 5, 9–10, 14, 54–5,
    63–6, 155–6, 173–5, 202–20
  see also fundamental performance
loyal/unloyal investors, concepts 63–5
LTIPs see long–term incentive plans

McKinsey 102, 107, 193, 225
management
  see also boards; chief ...; directors
  changes 3, 19, 24, 45–6, 72, 78–9, 158–62,
    171, 196–200, 202–3, 209–10, 229
  compensation 13, 41–3, 72, 78–9, 100–1,
    159–62, 196–200, 208–20, 226
  critique 2–5, 9–19, 40–6, 116–17, 121–2,
    124, 201–20
  'feel' judgements 121–2, 124, 191
  fiduciary duties 39–40, 117, 208–9
  governance issues 161, 192–3, 204–20, 237
  incentive schemes 13, 41–3, 72, 78–9,
    100–1, 159–62, 196–200, 216–20, 226
  index exit consequences 10–11, 45–6, 138
  LTIPs 42, 216–17
  meetings 34, 48–9, 63–6, 120–2, 136,
    141–2, 145, 151, 173, 187–200, 209–12,
    225
  misvaluation traps 4, 12–19, 23–5, 41–6,
    73–4, 82–117, 126–7
  performance measures 2–3, 9–10, 152
  'quality of management' 179, 201–20
  robust valuations 73–80, 81–117, 175–7
  self-valuations 73–80, 81–117, 145, 228
  shareprice maximisation crusades 2–5,
    9–19, 40–6, 71, 116–17, 166, 202–3, 212,
    217–18, 220, 237
  short-termism effectors 3–4, 9–19, 40–6,
    171, 175, 217–18
  STIPS 42, 216–17
  stock options 13–14, 41–3, 197, 216–20,
    226
  surveys 201–2
  VBM 11, 42–3, 72, 113, 217

management accounts 172–5
  see also accounting …
mandate lifetimes, fund managers 54–5,
  128–34, 138–9
market capitalisations 10–11, 49, 55–8,
  75–80, 84, 96–117, 166, 171–5
market makers 28
  see also house brokers
market share 155–6, 169, 173–5, 179–85
market system, concepts 26–7
market value 75–80, 84, 96–117, 171–5
  see also market capitalisations
marketing 1, 102–3, 156–7, 188–93, 200,
  218–20, 225–6
markets *see* financial markets
Marsh McClellan 107
mass communications 189–200
material movements, shareprices 129–34
mature businesses 204–5, 233–7
media 189
meetings 34, 48–9, 63–6, 120–2, 136, 141–2,
  145, 151, 173, 187–200, 209–12, 225
mergers and acquisitions (M&As) 12–14, 28,
  30, 41, 44, 71–2, 86, 108–9, 139, 153,
  179–85, 196–200, 204, 217–18
  see also takeovers
mindset changes, disclosures 171–5
minorities, fund managers 124–8
mission 9, 26–36, 144
mistrust issues 170–1, 185, 201–20
misvaluation traps
  acceptable limits 75–6, 99–100, 116–17
  concepts 4, 12–19, 21–5, 30–1, 34–8, 41–6,
    67, 72–4, 81–117, 126–7, 158–60, 175
  corrections 14–17, 21–5, 44–5, 158
  costs 14–15, 17, 43–6, 72, 84, 116–17
  cycles 12–19, 23–5, 41, 43–6, 72, 171
  growth/low–growth stocks 30–1
Moody's 202
mutual funds 233–4
Myners Report 207, 212–14

NASDAQ 23
net changes in individual holdings, value-
  determining shareholders 130–4, 160
net working capital, fair value strategy 108,
  110, 116
new entrants 173, 232–7
New York Stock Exchange 23
noise, shares-traded figures 124–5, 133
Nomination committees 208–9, 211, 214
non-disruptive value levers, concepts 158–62
non-executive directors 78–80, 159–62,
  190–200, 201–2, 207–20, 229
  see also boards
  governance issues 207–20
  statistics 208–10
non-financial performance measures,
  concepts 155–6, 169, 173–5, 179–84
notes, analysts 29–37, 82, 161, 189–91, 195,
  212

objectives, fair value 18–19
'old-economy' stocks 233–7

Omnicom 94
one-to-one communications 189–200
openness philosophies 166, 205–6
  see also disclosures
operating margins, fair value strategy 108,
  109–10, 116, 150–62, 179
operating measures 78–80, 98, 108, 109–10,
  116, 150–62, 169, 173–85
  see also fair- value levers
operational data, disclosure gaps 179–85
operations 1, 4–5
optimistic forecasts 90–1, 102–3, 115–16,
  151–2, 170, 196
options 13–14, 41–3, 60, 197, 216–20, 226
  see also derivatives
outsourcing, IR 5
overseas funds 38, 50–2, 61–2, 188, 235
overvaluations 4, 12–19, 21–5, 30–1, 35, 41–6,
  81–4, 116–17, 158, 164, 171–2, 196–7
  see also misvaluation …
Oxley–Sarbanes 29, 31

P&L accounts 106, 167–85
passive investors 36–40, 45–6, 51, 55–7,
  122–34
  see also index …
Pearson 94
pension funds 17, 26–7, 29–30, 36–40, 50–67,
  85, 233–4
  see also institutional investors
perceptions, investors 4–5, 45–6, 66, 77–80
perfect/imperfect markets, concepts 21–5,
  40–6, 73, 95
performance measures
  see also fair value levers; fundamental
    performance
  absolute value measures 84–117
  budgeting processes 100–1, 151–2
  cashflow 22, 25, 84–117, 179–84
  concepts 2–3, 9–10, 36–40, 53–8, 78–80,
    151–2, 155–6, 164, 202–20
  disclosures 164, 169, 173–85
  fund managers 36–40, 53–8
  IR 225–6
  management 2–3, 9–10, 152
  non-financial performance measures 155–6,
    169, 173–6, 179–84
  PEs 16, 23, 91–9, 152–3, 175
  relative value measures 84, 91–9, 152
perpetuity calculations 107–13, 155–6
PEs *see* price earnings ratios
poisoned chalices 40–3
pooled funds, fund managers 52–3
Porter, Michael 231–2
portfolio weightings, market caps 10, 55–6,
  58
PR 2, 13, 126, 187–200, 224
predictions 29–37, 41, 74, 77, 82, 86–117,
  121–34, 135–46, 149, 226–7
  see also forecasts
premiums
  misvaluation traps 12–19, 21–2, 23–5, 38,
    41–6, 73–4, 83–4, 116–17, 158
  risk premiums 87–8, 109, 114–15

presentations 124, 173, 188–200, 226–7
price earnings ratios (PEs) 16, 23, 91–9, 152–3
PricewaterhouseCoopers 156, 178
private equity, future prospects 236
product ratings, non-financial performance
    measures 155–6, 169, 173–6, 179–84
productivity issues 43, 155–6, 174, 179–84
profit-warning procedures 152–4, 161, 168–9
promotional events 192
proxy voting 47–50, 60, 121–2, 131
Prudential 127
pushed-down forecasts, benefits 105–6
quality controls, disclosures 179–84
'quality of management' 179, 201–20

R&D 86–7
ratings 16, 23, 29–31, 41, 72, 91–6, 98–9,
    102–3, 152–3
    see also price earnings ratio
re-ratings 15–16, 72, 98–9, 102–3, 152–4, 161
regulations 22, 29–31, 103, 142–3, 162, 164–7,
    179–85, 192–3, 207–8, 227, 232–7
relationships
    CEO roles 1–2, 18–19, 63–5, 71, 121–2,
        201–15
    CFO roles 101–2, 121–2, 136
    concepts 1–5, 18–19, 33–6, 40, 63–5, 74–5,
        119–34, 165, 201–20, 223–9
    CRM 192, 204
    fund managers 2, 29–30, 33–6, 40, 63–5, 75,
        119–34, 165, 201–20, 223–9
    IR 2–5, 18–19, 22–3, 34, 40, 48–9, 74–5, 89,
        101–3, 117, 136, 145, 156–7, 177,
        187–200, 223–9
relative value measures 16, 23, 84, 91–9,
    152–3, 175
remuneration, management 13, 41–3, 72,
    78–9, 100–1, 159–62, 196–200, 208–20,
    226
remuneration committees 208–9, 211, 214
Rentokil 126
retail investors 48–9, 57
return on equity, cost of capital 113–14
returns links, disclosures 178
revenue growth 108–9, 150–62, 169–70,
    179–80
    see also earnings . . .
reverse-engineering, short–term performance
    13–14
rights issues 12–13, 28–9
risk 85, 87–116, 183–4
risk-free interest rates, CAPM 87–116
roadshows 188, 191, 224
robust valuations, concepts 73–80, 81–117,
    175–7
rumours 195

S&P 500 10
SBUs *see* strategic business units
sectors 11–12, 92–6, 114, 121
segmentation uses, investors 52, 66–7
self-interrogations, disclosures 178–80
self-regulations 208–20

self-valuations, management 73–80, 81–117,
    145, 228
sell-side analysts 26, 29–37, 74, 82, 89–90,
    102–3, 145, 150–1, 169–70, 174–5, 181–4,
    196, 199–200, 234–7
    see also brokers
    biases 29–37, 39, 82, 117, 170, 196
    forecasts 29–37, 41, 82, 89–90, 102–3,
        150–1, 174–8, 196, 199–200, 234–5
    future prospects 235–6
    notes 29–37, 82, 161, 189–91, 195, 212
    power issues 33–4, 102–3, 151
    roles 26, 29–37, 102–3, 150–1, 169–70,
        174–5, 236
    statistics 30–1
    system overview 26
shareprices 2–5, 9–19, 21–2, 23–5, 31–2, 38,
    40, 41–6, 50–1, 59–63, 67, 72, 73–4,
    81–117, 126–7, 129, 133, 143–4, 158–60,
    171, 175, 176, 234–5
    cyclical inevitability 3–4, 12–18, 23–5, 41,
        43–6, 72, 129, 171
    directional traders 40, 47–8, 58–63, 76–80,
        119–34, 227–9
    discounts 44–5, 73–4, 83, 116–17, 158
    material movements 129–34
    maximisation crusades 2–5, 9–19, 40–6, 71,
        116–17, 166, 202–3, 212, 217–18, 220,
        237
    misvaluation traps 4, 12–19, 21–2, 23–5,
        38, 41–6, 67, 73–4, 81–117, 126–7,
        158–60, 175
    PEs 16, 23, 91–9, 152–3, 175
    premiums 12–19, 23–5, 38, 73–4, 83–4,
        116–17, 158
    value-determining shareholders 76–80,
        119–34
shareholder registers 4–5, 18–19, 34–5, 47–50,
    67, 125–34, 219–20, 225, 227–9, 234
    see also investors
    account management 66–7, 77, 136–46,
        227–9
    analysis needs 4–5, 18–19, 34–5, 47–50, 67,
        125–34, 219–20, 225, 227–9
    competitor analysis 144–6
    net changes in individual holdings 130–4,
        160
shareholder value 9–10
shares-traded figures 98–9, 124–34, 160
    net changes in individual holdings 130–4,
        160
    value-determining shareholders 129–34,
        160
Shell 170–1
short-term incentive plans (STIPs) 42, 216–17
short-termism 3–4, 9–19, 35–6, 40–6, 54–6,
    71–2, 154–6, 217–18
skills needs 4–5
softing practices 29–30, 39–40
speculation 15–16
spin-offs 30
staff issues 43, 155–6, 173–4, 179–84, 223–5,
    237
Standard and Poor's 202

start-ups 'sappling' strategies 72
STIPs *see* short-term incentive plans
stock markets 2–3, 142–3, 164, 192–3, 232–3
   see also financial markets
   historical background 232–3
stock options, management 13–14, 41–3, 197,
   216–20, 226
strategic business units (SBUs) 42–3, 107,
   112–13, 172
strategy 1, 3–5, 18–19, 22–3, 46, 54, 67,
   71–80, 100–17, 145–6, 147–220, 223–9
   changes 78–9, 158–62, 196–200, 204–5, 229
   communications 193–200, 223–9
   coordination 5, 18–19, 79–80, 161–2,
     187–200, 223–9
   cycles 3, 54, 72–3, 101, 104–5, 216–18
   disclosure gaps 179–85
   fair value 4–5, 18–19, 46, 67, 71–80,
     100–17, 145–6, 147–220, 231–7
   fund managers 56, 120–1, 141
stretch budgets 151–2
substitute investors 77–8, 143–6
substitute technology 173, 232–7
suppliers 173, 232–7
surveys, management 201–2
synergies 44, 112–13

tacit information, concepts 136
takeovers 12, 17, 41, 44, 71–2, 139, 153,
   179–85, 217–18
   see also mergers . . .
taxation 64, 84–5, 92, 116, 150, 172
terminal years, fair value 109–11
timing of releases 78–9, 159–62
   see also fair value levers
total shareholder returns (TSRs) 11–12, 16,
   41–2, 72, 214–18, 233–4
track records 202–5
tracker funds 55–63, 125
   see also index . . .
training 72, 105
transparency issues 30
Treasury Notes 87–8
triggers category, account management
   138–46
trust issues 170–1, 185, 201–20
trustees, pension funds 26
TSRs *see* total shareholder returns

underperforming divisions 164
undervaluations 16–18, 21–5, 30–1, 44–6, 61,
   81–4, 116–17, 142, 158–60, 184–5, 196–7
   see also misvaluation . . .
unit trusts 26–7, 233–4
   see also institutional investors
United States (US) 30–1, 48, 60, 103, 188,
   207–8
unloyal investors, concepts 63–5

valuations
   absolute value measures 84–117
   CAPM 22, 86, 87–116
   cashflow measures 22, 25, 84–117, 179–84
   component parts 73–80, 81–117

   concepts 84–117
   financial models 107–17
   methods 4–5, 12–19, 73–80, 84–117
   misvaluation traps 4, 12–19, 21–2, 23–5,
     30–1, 34–8, 41–6, 67, 72–4, 81–117,
     126–7, 158–60, 175
   overvaluations 4, 12–19, 21–5, 30–1, 35,
     41–6, 81–4, 116–17, 158, 171–2, 196–7
   PEs 16, 23, 91–9, 152–3, 175
   premiums 12–19, 21–2, 23–5, 38, 41–6,
     73–4, 83–4, 116–17, 158
   relative value measures 84, 91–9, 152
   rules 103–6
   self-valuations 73–80, 81–117, 145, 228
   undervaluations 16–18, 21–5, 30–1, 44–6,
     61, 81–4, 116–17, 142, 158–60, 184–5,
     196–7
   WACC 42–3, 87–117, 179–84
value-based management (VBM) 11, 42–3, 72,
   113, 217
value drivers, VBM 42–3, 217
value levers *see* fair value levers
value story, concepts 155–6, 175–8, 199–200
value-determining shareholders
   see also active investors; directional
     traders
   account management 136–46, 227–9
   behaviour prediction processes 74, 77,
     135–46, 149, 226–7
   characteristics 128–9
   communication methods 156–62, 194–200,
     227–9
   concepts 76–80, 119–34, 135–46, 180, 219,
     227–9
   coopting practices 141–6, 190–200
   disclosures 178–85
   identification processes 128–34, 180, 227–9
   levers assessment processes 74, 77–80,
     149–200
   minority influences 124–8
   motivations 135–46
   net changes in individual holdings 130–4,
     160
   profiling processes 74, 77, 135–46, 226–9
   shares-traded figures 129–34, 160
   substitute investors 77–8, 143–6
VBM *see* value-based management
Vodafone 94, 170
volatility 19, 60, 87–8, 114–16, 175–6, 234
vulnerabilities category, account
   management 138–46
vulture funds 59–60

WACC *see* weighted average cost of capital
Wall Street 2
wealth maximisation 9–10
websites 165, 187–200, 224, 226
weighted average cost of capital (WACC)
   42–3, 87–117, 179–84
working capital 86, 106, 108, 110, 116
WorldCom 167, 206
WPP 94
write-downs, overvalued assets 164